Parisian Views

Shelley Rice

Parisian Views

Shelley Rice

The MIT Press

Cambridge, Massachusetts

London, England

This book was set in Sabon by Graphic Composition, Inc.
Printed and bound in the United States of America.

Library of Congress Cataloging-in-Publication Data

Rice, Shelley.

    Parisian views / Shelley Rice.

       p.   cm.

    Includes bibliographical references and index.

    ISBN 0-262-18184-3 (alk. paper)

    1. Photography—France—Paris—History—19th century.   2. Paris
(France)—History—1848–1870.   3. Haussmann, Georges Eugène, baron,
1809–1891—Contributions in urban renewal.   I. Title.

TR72.P37R53   1997

779'.9944'3609034—dc21   97-7986

                                                                  CIP

To Charles, with love and thanks

Contents

Illustrations

I   Introduction: Time Zones

II   Parisian Views

List of Illustrations

Preface

"Time Zones" is an adaptation of an essay first published in *Paris et le Daguerreotype,* an exhibition at the Musée Carnavelet in Paris in 1989. The original, and very different, version of "Parisian Views" won the Logan Award for New Writing on Photography, and was therefore published in the magazine of the Photographic Resource Center in Boston in 1986, and reprinted in their book *Multiple Views,* edited by Daniel P. Younger. Both "Still Points in a Turning World" and "On Camels and Cathedrals" (initially titled "Focus: Notre-Dame"), in somewhat different forms, made their public debuts in *Afterimage,* in May, 1987 and February 1990. "Souvenirs" appeared in *Art in America* in September 1988. The author wishes to thank these publications for their support.

Acknowledgments

T his book has been a major part of my life for more than ten years: it has, in large measure, determined my movements, my friends and even my thoughts. So the shape of this volume, slim though it is, is the shape of a large chunk of my adulthood, and in acknowledging those who aided me in my intellectual pursuits I am, simultaneously, thanking my friends, colleagues, and loved ones for helping me to make a life.

There are, of course, those people, both friends and esteemed colleagues, who helped me to penetrate "les mystères de Paris," by aiding me with my lodgings, my accent, my library cards, my social *savoir faire,* my banking, and my intellectual development: Raymond Bellour, Anne-Marie Duguet and Philippe Martelet, Molly Nesbit, Kenneth Silver, Peter Galassi, Peter Bunnell, Françoise and Elizabeth Reynaud, Michel Frizot, and Annick Bruchet among others. Then there are the professional connections that sometimes turned into valued friendships: Marie de Thézy and Jean-Paul Avice of the Bibliothèque Historique, Martine d'Astier, Pierre Borhan and the staff at the Mission du Patrimoine Photographique, Jean-Luc Monterosso and his colleagues at Paris Audiovisuel, Alain Desvergnes and everyone at the Ecole Nationale de la Photographie in Arles, Geneviève Acker and Pierre Collambert of the Fulbright Commission, Jean-Claude Lemagny and Bernard Marbot at the Bibliothèque Nationale, Françoise Heilbrun and the late Philippe Néagu of the Musée d'Orsay, scholar and writer Tony Sutcliffe, Flammarion editor Suzanne Tise, and writer and editor Michel Winock among them. By and large, working in France—on this book and other projects—has been a pleasure for me, and I have all of the above people and their co-workers (especially at the Bibliothèque Nationale, the Biblio-thèque Historique de la Ville de Paris, and the Musée Carnavalet) to thank for that.

One influence bears a special mention and a special thanks: that of Marshall Berman, whose book *All That Is Solid Melts into Air* catapulted me somehow into the nineteenth century. My debt to him is enormous, and all these pages bear the imprint of his thought about the clashing cultures that together define the modern urban experience.

As for money: people have been extremely generous in support of this project. I wish to thank, most especially, the Fulbright Commission, the Guggenheim Foundation, and the Hasselblad Center in Sweden for the grants that made extended periods of work in Paris possible. But thanks also must go to the PEN/American Center for the PEN/Jerard Award, the Photographic Resource Center in Boston for the Logan Award, the Rockefeller Foundation for the residency in their Bellagio villa, the National Endowment for the Humanities for two Travel to Collection Grants, the French Minister of Culture for a "bourse d'étude" that paid my way in Paris for a while, and all of my French colleagues who found "gigs" for me that funded my frequent trips to the City of Light.

Then, of course, I have to thank loved ones, mainly for putting up with my French obsessions and my frequent absences:

my parents, and Emory and David, especially, deserve kisses for their patience and fortitude; acknowledgment must also go to Emory Craig for his editing, both of my manuscripts and my ideas, for over a decade. Patient too were all of my colleagues and friends at New York University and the School of Visual Arts, who covered for me when I was gone and graciously tolerated my interest in dead artists. Special thanks are owed to Betsey Kershaw and Erin Donnelly, for typing and copy editing my manuscript, and Jon Kline, for both editing and photographic work. All these people, along with Carlos and Asia de Jesus, Lorie Novak, Nancy Goldring, Walter and Cecile Abish, Barbara Novak, Robert Rosenblum, Irving Sandler, Jayne Baum, Phyllis Galembo and Chief Nosa, Brian Wood, Betsy Baker and Ted Mooney at *Art in America*, my literary agents Elaine Markson and Mary Kling, and Roger Conover, Jim McWethy, and Sandra Minkkinen at The MIT Press, kept me moving by cheering me on, and shaming me into finishing what I started.

Parisian Views

I

Introduction: Time Zones

T he date is 1838, or maybe 1839; the time, about 8:00 A.M. Louis Jacques Mandé Daguerre is in his studio facing the Boulevard du Temple, working as he has been for about fourteen years to discover the secret of permanently capturing the image in the camera obscura. Looking down at the street several floors below, he focuses his camera in the hopes of freezing the Parisian life around him into the stop-time of a photograph.

His experiment succeeds, and the result is the daguerreotype in the collection of the Stadtmuseum in Munich *(fig. 1.¹)*. Directly below are the roofs of the buildings in the immediate vicinity and the views (seen in reverse, of course) of the houses that line the street. Curving off to the left, the boulevard moves back into deep space, to disappear in the middle rear of the picture. The signs of people are everywhere: in the residences with their awnings and shutters, in the orderly arrangement of the trees lining the sidewalk, in the signs of commerce that exist all around. But of people themselves, there is only one, who is not quite completely drawn *(fig. 1.²)*.

fig 1.[1]

L. J. M. Daguerre, *Boulevard du Temple,* 1838 (Stadtmuseum, Munich)

fig 1.[2]

Detail of *fig. 1.*[1]

fig 1.[3]

L. J. M. Daguerre, *Boulevard du Temple*, 1838 (Stadtmuseum, Munich)

This singular gentleman, who alone among the passersby on the Boulevard du Temple stood still long enough to have his image impressed during the 20- to 30-minute exposure time, fascinated the American Samuel F. B. Morse, who described this daguerreotype in a letter to his brother on March 7, 1839: "The Boulevard, so constantly filled with a moving throng of pedestrians and carriages, was perfectly solitary, except an individual who was having his boots brushed. His feet were compelled, of course, to be stationary for some time, one being on the box of the boot black, and the other one on the ground. Consequently his boots and legs were well defined, but he is without body or head, because these were in motion." [1]

This points up something that is too easily forgotten: that a photograph is an *event* transformed into an object. Rather than being a record of *things,* as we often suppose, it is the fixing of light in space over *time.* Daguerre himself, it seems, was aware of this; this particular image exists in at least two versions, each of them recording the scene at a different time *(fig. 1.*[3]*).* The early French photographers, in general, showed more signs than photographers in our own day of being interested in the temporal ramifications of the medium. Hippolyte Bayard's serial images of statues and buildings, Henri Le Secq's cinematic renditions of cathedrals from close-up to detailed views, Charles Marville's repetitions of the same pictorial structure in his photographs of Paris streets: all bespeak preoccupations with time and perception that were to flower later in the chronophotographs of Etienne Jules Marey, the serial paintings of Claude Monet, and the philosophy of Henri Bergson. We tend nowadays, caught up as we are in a photographic technology that works faster than the eye can see and an art market focused on pictures as precious objects, to be less likely to notice the temporal paradoxes that presented themselves to the earliest image makers. But these daguerreotypes, reflecting as they do the magic of photography in its most primitive form, force us to confront, once again, this seminal aspect of the medium.

For as Morse's comment makes abundantly clear, Daguerre's picture of Paris from his window does not, under any circumstances, show us what he saw as he stood looking down at the street that day. Daguerre's Paris was *crowded;* the migrations into the city of workers from the countryside during the first half of the nineteenth century caused a population explosion that was building into a crisis situation. The boundaries of the city had not yet been extended (as they would be in 1860), and the 1836 census recorded a population in the city center of 899,913.[2] This crush of people gave rise to traffic problems that Charles Baudelaire would describe, in the 1850s, as a nightmare: "Just now, . . . I was crossing the boulevard in a great hurry, splashing through the mud in the midst of a seething chaos, with death galloping at me from every side."[3] His description was certainly applicable to a main thoroughfare like the Boulevard du Temple, which at the time housed Daguerre's popular Diorama (a panoramic painted picture show, like those discussed in chapter 4, but enlivened by changing light effects) as well as numerous cafés and theaters, like the Funambules, the Gaîté, and the Cirque Olympique, whose melodramatic presentations had given this street the nickname "le Boulevard du Crime."

Yet none of this activity is evident in our daguerreotype, in spite of its miraculous detail. "Objects moving are not impressed," Morse wrote.[4] The early camera apparatus recorded only what *endured.* This "mirror of nature" could reflect only a slow-time universe from which human activity was excluded. That would soon change: by 1841, thanks to Antoine Claudet, portraits were possible, and the decades of the 1850s and 1860s saw "instantaneous" photographs produced with Frederick Scott Archer's wet collodion process. But in 1838, Daguerre gave us this magical image of a time frame that did not coincide with his own experience—that existed parallel to his (and our) temporal dimension. And it has come down to us as incontrovertible evidence that our world is created temporally as well as spatially: that Paris is a time as well as a place.

So we, in regarding this picture over a century and a half later, are in a position parallel to Daguerre's own. We too are in a different time frame, standing in the same Parisian space but looking through a temporal window that cannot be traversed. We, of course, are much farther removed from this visual event than the artist himself, because we are looking across a century and a half of historical time. Much has happened to Paris since this picture was taken. Not long afterward, from 1853 to 1869, Baron Haussmann, prefect of the Seine, would transform the city by piercing the wide boulevards and straight streets that were the core of Napoleon III's urban renewal plan.

Such a massive transformation, followed as it has been by successive if less all-encompassing projects that continue into our own day, means that many of the buildings and streets depicted in early daguerreotypes no longer exist. But these images, with their minute detail, are still with us—our first proof, as Roland Barthes has said, that "the past is as certain as the present."[5]

Because we are looking at these pictures across a chasm of historical change, we tend to see them today through a fog of nostalgia. We marvel at architecture we can no longer touch and dream about life stories, now over, that we can never know. We sigh about an Old Paris and a style of living that we perceive as slower, smaller, saner, and somehow more human than our own. But we should beware: such ideas are a thoroughly modern construct. When Baudelaire wrote, during the Second Empire, that "Old Paris is gone (no human heart/changes half so fast as a city's face)," he was helping to bring this romantic idea of the past into being.[6] The traumatic convulsions of the city's spaces and population, the destruction of traditions and the traces of history under Haussmann, gave rise to a nostalgia for *what was* that we cling to even in our own day. "Anything about which one knows that one soon will not have it around becomes an image," wrote Walter Benjamin.[7] These early photographs are, for us, that image of Balzac's world, or the streets of *La Bohème*.

But that attachment to the narrow passages and crumbling stones of Old Paris was not shared by most people living there in the 1830s and 1840s. When photographing the city, the early daguerreotypists almost never chose as their subject the streets that would, in later decades, make Marville's and Jean-Eugène-Auguste Atget's hearts quicken. There was a practical reason for this: the lack of sunlight in these cavernous spaces, best described by M. Lachaise in his medical topography of the period. "Because of the crowding of the buildings, and their excessive height," he wrote, "the sun can penetrate only a short while in some streets, unevenly in others, and never in most, and so on the first floor one is always in the dark, even though the sun is already high on the horizon."[8] Balzac himself, writing about the *quartier* around La Grève and the Hôtel de Ville, noticed that "the inhabitants, who during the month of June light their lamps at 5:00 in the evening, never extinguish them in the winter."[9]

But there was another reason, besides the lack of light, for the daguerreotypists' lack of interest in quaint old streets: most Parisians during these years perceived them as dirty, crowded, and unhealthy. Covered with mud and makeshift shanties, damp and fetid, filled with the signs of poverty as well as the garbage and waste left there by the inadequate and faulty sewer system, these narrow roads hardly seemed worth celebrating in jewellike, metallic "sun pictures." "How ugly Paris seems after a year's absence," wrote the Vicomte de Launay in 1838. "How one chokes in these dark, narrow and dank corridors that we like to call the streets of Paris! One would think that one was in a subterranean city, that's how heavy is the atmosphere, how profound is the darkness! . . . And thousands of men live, act and press against each other in these liquid shadows, like reptiles in a swamp."[10] Their mistrust of these squalid streets was not misplaced: disease spread like wildfire through filthy, overpopulated neighborhoods, as the cholera epidemics of 1832 (which killed 18,400 people, including the prime minister) and 1848–1849 (in which 19,000 Parisians died) made clear.[11] Later inhabitants might approve or disapprove of what Haussmann did with the streets of the city, but most people at the time would have agreed with Maxime Du Camp that "After 1848, Paris was about to become uninhabitable."[12]

Given these attitudes, it hardly seems reasonable to regard these early image makers only as preservers of the precious past. These photographers were also harbingers of the future — of both Paris and visual imagery. These early photographs are the building blocks in a modern vision that has changed the world. Our own media society, in fact, rests squarely on the shoulders of these tiny traces of history. Daguerreotypes are one-of-a-kind images; jewellike and rare, they seem remote from the reproductions in newspapers and magazines that inundate us every day. By their very uniqueness, these pictures rest on the threshold of modernity, with one foot in the aesthetically elite past and one in the imagistically democratic future. (Understanding the connections between the political and the aesthetic ramifications of the medium long before Walter Benjamin, the photographer Etienne Carjat wrote a poem celebrating Daguerre's invention as the first step toward "L'Art du Pauvre.")[13] All of the Frenchmen who picked up a camera in those early days saw themselves as pioneers, on the forefront of a wave of progressive national liberalism that had prompted the statesman François Arago to suggest that the country purchase this invention in order to offer it freely to the world. These men were the first to shape a pictorial vision that held in balance both the raw materials of history and the eye perceiving them, and they knew they were breaking new ground.

The invention of photography came at that privileged moment when art and science, technology and aesthetics joined forces on a common path. As Daguerre worked, the scientific world view was on the ascendancy; in art, the foundations were being laid for Gustave Courbet and the Realist school. The writings of this period make it clear that Daguerre's contemporaries were most impressed with his invention's ability to capture "reality": these "sun pictures" were seen by his colleagues as direct transcripts of God's creations, transparent and authorless reproductions "equal to nature itself."[14] But even now, as we read these texts and marvel at their naiveté, we can look at the pictures and see that the artists themselves were struggling with questions much more complex than the "mirror of nature" analogy would allow. They were struggling to define their city in images—over a decade before Baron Haussmann would do so in fact.

This is an important point, and one that is not often enough made. We are used to seeing photographs as history, as evidence of the past. Roland Barthes, in *Camera Lucida*, eloquently described the perception of a photograph as a kind of death, a stop-time that flows not forward but "back from presentation to retention."[15] Yet this early period of French photography makes manifest another layer of complexity, of temporal and spatial reality, that cannot be adequately explained by this formula. The image makers describing Paris during the mid-nineteenth century were, like Haussmann, forging a new visual image of the city parallel to the prefect's own; whether working on commission or on their own, they too were shaping urban space, in two dimensions as opposed to three. And, interestingly enough, these new visions, as if possessed of a certain clairvoyance, appeared years before the construction crews arrived, making these pictures a kind of magic mirror through which the then Parisian future can be dimly perceived.

Photographers were, of course, not the only ones to define the Paris-of-the-imagination before the new City of Light (so named in honor of the newly installed gas lighting) existed in fact. Looking at some of these early sun pictures, one can agree with T. J. Clark that Haussmann himself merely realized, in time and space and matter, changes that had been both anticipated and described by commentators for thirty years. Clark quotes Victor Hugo, looking down from the tower of Notre-Dame at the bourse and the Rue de Rivoli in 1830 and seeing in his mind's eye a vision of the city that Paris would indeed become several decades later:

> Let us add that if it is right that the architecture of an edifice be adapted to its purpose in such a way that the purpose be readable from the edifice's exterior alone, we can never be sufficiently amazed at a monument that can equally well be a royal palace, a house of commons, a town hall, a college, a riding school, an academy, an entrepot, a tribunal, a museum, a barracks, a sepulcher, a temple, a theater. For the time being it is a stock exchange. . . . We have that colonnade going round the monument, under which on the great days of religious observance there can be developed in majestic style the theories of stockbrokers and commission agents.
>
> Without a doubt these are quite superb monuments. Add to them a quantity of handsome streets, amusing and varied like the Rue de Rivoli, and I do not despair that Paris, seen from a balloon, should one day present that richness of line, that opulence of detail, that diversity of aspect, that hint of the grandiose in the simple and the unexpected in the beautiful, which characterizes a checkerboard.[16]

In terms of Paris's ultimate fate, it seems that the handwriting was on the wall years before Haussmann took office—and writers like Hugo and Balzac, who also announced, in *Les Petits Bourgeois*, that "the old Paris is passing," were not the only ones to read the signs.[17] The photographers who picked up their cameras, those novel proofs of technological ingenuity and progress, both before and during the Second Empire, used these instruments to visualize not only the city that existed before their eyes but also the one that would be coming into being: the city that would be the arena for modern traffic, mass immigration, department stores, train stations, and hot air balloons. Looking at the rare panoramic daguerreotypes, or pre-Haussmann photographic documents like Henri Le Secq's *Album Berger* in the Bibliothèque Historique de la Ville de Paris, one gets the distinct sense that this new metropolis existed as an idea construction, a vision in the heads of artists and writers, years before the prefect's workers created it with their machines and labor in the physical world.

On this level, these images—which are indeed photographic traces, evidence of cityscapes that definitely existed in the material environment when the pictures were made—are also visionary creations. Le Secq's *Album Berger,* for example, is one of the more romantic eulogies to the passing Paris—created years before what we consider the actual passing to have occurred. In 1853, when the artist produced this album from photographs taken between 1849 and 1853 *(figs. 1.[4], 1.[6], 1.[7], 1.[8])*, Haussmann was just taking office; the survey map that would be the basis for the construction process was still to be done, and it would be quite some time before Napoleon III's plan would start to redefine in a global way the physical spaces and lifestyles of the City of Light. But Le Secq's work is nevertheless a dirge: filled with demolitions, with destructions, with ruins, it is an elegy to a disappearance that, in historical terms, had not yet occurred on a widespread scale. Like Hugo's statements, based as they were on the Bourse and the still incomplete Rue de Rivoli, these pictures are an extrapolation: from specific pieces of evidence, they project a doom-laden vision of the future.

Also like Hugo, Le Secq was correct in his assessments: the particular demolitions he photographed were indeed the harbingers of things to come, and by 1860 all of Paris, it seemed, would look this way. But what does such an understanding do to our certainty that these images reflect only the past, the evidence of our history? What happens when we begin to grapple with the strange shifting of tenses that occurs when we look at photographs not only as traces of the past but also as pre-visions of the future?

Once again, Barthes's perceptions in *Camera Lucida* are relevant here. Regarding a picture taken by Alexander Gardner in the jail cell of Lewis Payne, who tried to assassinate Secretary of State W. H. Seward in nineteenth-century America, Barthes wrote: "The photograph is handsome, as is the boy . . . but . . . he is going to die. I read at the same time: *this will be* and *this has been;* I observe with horror an anterior future of which death is the stake. By giving me the absolute past of the pose, the photograph tells me death in the future. . . . I shudder . . . over a catastrophe which has already occurred. Whether or not the subject is already dead, every photograph is this catastrophe." [18] Le Secq's *Album Berger* is, indeed, this catastrophe: a *this will be* merged with a *this has been* in such a way that it becomes impossible to separate the past from a future that, simultaneous with being predicted, has already occurred.

Barthes considered this hallucinatory shifting of tenses, this bizarre distortion of temporal realities, to be the "madness" of photography. He is right, of course; and this madness is something that is taken so thoroughly for granted in our society that we notice it no longer. Inherent in these photographs, these traces of the "real" world, are the history of Paris, of France; the destruction of the traditions inherent in the physical structure of a city; and the feelings of this artist about this event. Poised on the verge of massive change, Le Secq's Paris becomes very dear, and this man's reactions were not his alone. For even though many Parisians were aware that their city no longer worked, that its mud and mire were both deadly and difficult, they were not psychologically prepared to accept the cataclysmic changes necessary to bring their town into the modern world. Haussmann's work, accomplished in large measure within a period of

fig 1.[4]
H. Le Secq, *Tour St. Jacques*, 1853, from the *Album Berger*
(Bibliothèque Historique de la Ville de Paris, Paris)

fig 1.[5]

Anonymous, *Panorama taken from the Tour St. Jacques,* 1867
(Bibliothèque Historique de la Ville de Paris, Paris)

less than twenty years, gave rise to nostalgia and ambivalence, excitement and pain. Like the excavations that laid the foundations for new buildings and simultaneously uncovered the historical remnants of the old, the prefect's constructions reached into the subterranean depths not only of the earth but also of human emotions. These pictures are records of these depths, now paved over with parking lots. Like Cassandra's prophecies, they bespeak a destiny that might have been necessary but was not for that reason either easy or desirable.

Le Secq's visionary album is about the inevitability of this destiny and his recognition that, henceforth, his memories of Paris would have no counterpart in the actual structures of his environment. Like Baudelaire's poems, these images embody Walter Benjamin's definition of *spleen,* which "places centuries between the present moment and the time actually being lived." [19] It is, perhaps, this separation of memory from fact, this demolition of the collective personal and public mythologies inherent in city spaces, that is the real tragedy, the "catastrophe," in the photography of Haussmannization. In a work like this one, the stasis of memory comes up against the crushing speed of historical change, and it is inevitably vanquished. Le Secq has transformed his world into a frozen photographic allegory in order to preserve it—but images like these, while recording the traces of the past, can do nothing to prevent the future they simultaneously predict: the alienation of modern metropolises, the restlessness of the freeways of Los Angeles, the continually demolished skyscrapers of New York, and the mobility of twentieth-century lives lost in space.

These chapters attempt to see these pictures as the allegories of our social history, evidence of a past that implies a future. The Parisian views described within this book, all of them sun pictures faithfully transcribing the mirror of nature, are in this sense luminous objects that radiate back and forth between time zones these texts try to describe. These studies, on that level, should be perceived as a series of archaeological digs, of piercing looks through the frames of images in order to uncover the layers of time and space they reveal. The chapters are independent of each other, though interrelationships between their various themes abound; there is, deliberately, no overriding narrative here, because this was a period in which the various temporal and spatial layers of life interpenetrated in ways that were often as complex as the Barthesian *noeme* of a photo.

It is no accident that photography itself came of age during this historical moment when the madness of modern life became manifest in the consciousness and lives of Parisian artists and writers. On a certain level, the lack of narrative in the stop-time of a photograph—that frozen, dumb transcription of reality that is, ultimately, a fragment of time and space that defies all earlier concepts of global meaning—echoes the lack of a defined world view that characterizes this historical period. Early French photography is a universe of bits and pieces; strung together, all of these various images shimmering as they do with layers of time and light, create a constantly shifting collage whose interrelationships form a network as complicated and as new as Haussmann's arteries of streets. The demolitions of neighborhoods and lifestyles inherent in the rebuilding of Paris allowed artists to see this city not in its organic wholeness as before but as bits and pieces every bit as existentially isolated as the freeze-frame of a photograph. In a sense, both photography and the renovated metropolis were destroyers of meaning, calling into question all the assumptions that had come before; and these chapters are about the deconstruction and reconstruction of the urban environment, whether physical or mental, in two dimensions or three.

To explain: take, for instance, the Tour St. Jacques, depicted by Le Secq *(fig. 1.*[4]*)*. Once a part of a church, St. Jacques de la Boucherie, the tower here stands alone, the recently remaindered morsel of an architectural structure whose ecclesiastical function had linked it—in form as well as function—to the community in a specific, clearly defined way. Forlorn and phallic, the tower remains as an object (art for art's sake, as it were), its community function destroyed to underline its interesting historical and architectural shape. Later, under Haussmann's direction, this building would undergo even further change: the small hill from which it grows in this image would be leveled by the prefect, it would be transplanted (so to speak) in order to make its presence on the extended Rue de Rivoli more compatible with the urbanist's aesthetic and geometric aims. Although, to this day, a distinctive part of Paris's urban environment, the tower lost its original purpose and meaning during the mid-nineteenth century; becoming a fragment, yet another bit of the collage the city was to become, it took its place—with form but in a sense without content—on the checkerboard of Victor Hugo's imagination.

It is not necessary to belabor this point, that formerly stable objects, social symbols, and behavior patterns became floating *signs* in Haussmann's Paris; this perception has become commonplace in scholarly writings about this period. What is important here, however, is the link that exists between the tower-without-a-meaning and early French photographs. They too wrenched objects, spaces, and people out of their moorings in space and time, leaving them floating without narrative support in the increasingly complex checkerboard of the modern image network. As depicted in the numerous photographs that exist from this époque, Parisian monuments lose all semblance of stable, community content and begin to splinter into signs whose shifting meanings are entirely dependent on the eye of the operator/beholder. Everything in Haussmann's city became an open-ended perspective, a point of view that could be captured, piecemeal, by a camera; and the sum total of the photographs that exist leave us with a broken narrative whose meanings have been rebuilt for us only in this multiplicity of subjective fragments.

Le Secq's tower, for instance, is the sad remnant of a passing era. Other image makers, however, reveling in its height, climbed to the top of the Tour St. Jacques in order to register a panoramic overview of their town *(fig. 1.⁵)*, in a celebration of modernism that links an old monument with the vision inherent in hot air balloons, survey maps, and trains. The shifting position of the tower within the continuum of urban space signified, as well, a restructuring of its temporal ramifications: its very existence historically, its physical presence, let it become a piece of the always unfinished puzzle that links the past to the present and future in the archaeological dig of old European cities that have survived into modern times. Streets are restructured, some buildings are demolished and others restored; and each change imperceptibly alters our perception of historical time while simultaneously altering the habits of our daily lives. Seen in this larger, experiential context, the tower itself, like a photograph, is eternally trapped in a time warp, a radiating movement between tenses that, by definition, can never be resolved.

Roland Barthes saw photography as the rupture in time that "divides the history of the world." [20] He was referring to the advent of photographic evidence: our certainty of the past because it has left its indisputable mark, our inability, from this moment on, to reject the specificities of our history. But I am referring to another, related division—the rupture in our concept of time that occurred with the advent of modernism, which is discussed so eloquently by John Berger and Jean Mohr in their book *Another Way of Telling*.[21] This was the era when the concentric circles of time—cosmic/geological, historical, personal—ceased to stay in their age-old places, to rotate in the traditional patterns of relationship that securely anchored our finite lives within the framework of the infinite. This was the moment, this Age of Revolutions, when historical events changed faster than individual lives; when cities altered their faces more rapidly than people did and fell into ruins before human bodies had time to age; when the personal itself, subjective time, became the measure of all things almost by default, for lack of a yardstick against which one could gauge the idea of progress. It is the era when the particularities of history became important because they gave people something, at least, to hold on to, however provisionally—when the stop-time of a photograph, therefore, became like the Dutch boy's finger in the dike.

What pops up continually in these chapters—whether about Paris itself, or the trains that brought people there—is the extreme tension between the exigencies of subjective time and the particularities of social history that marks this period. The rupture, the catastrophe that was Haussmannization made manifest the destruction of the unity of the self-in-history that was still, at this moment, an expectation of life. On a certain level, the French have never recovered from this trauma. Paris today, a modern metropolis filled with cars, TGVs, fax machines, and sophisticated media, is still a city whose identity is deeply rooted

fig 1.[6]

H. Le Secq, *Demolitions, Place de l'Hôtel de Ville*, 1853, from the *Album Berger*
(Bibliothèque Historique de la Ville de Paris, Paris)

fig 1.[7]
H. Le Secq, *Demolitions, rue St. Martin,* 1853, from the *Album Berger*
(Bibliothèque Historique de la Ville de Paris, Paris)

fig 1.[8]

H. Le Secq, *Place du Carrousel,* 1852, from the *Album Berger*
(Bibliothèque Historique de la Ville de Paris, Paris)

fig 1.[9]
E. Baldus, *Place du Carrousel, Palais des Tuileries*, n.d. (c. 1860)
(Bibliothèque Nationale, Paris)

in the nineteenth century, as if on some imperceptible emotional level the stress-
ful change imposed on inhabitants during this *époque* stopped the flow of time
even as history itself marched on — as if the stop-time of a photograph, that
backward flow from presentation to retention, became an inescapable mode of
life. Jean-Paul Sartre's description of Baudelaire, that "he chose to advance back-
wards with his face turned toward the past, crouching on the floor of the car
that was taking him away with his eyes fixed on the disappearing road," may
describe a social reality rather than a purely personal one.[22]

Baudelaire is, perhaps, the best gauge of this traumatic temporal earth-
quake, of the upheavals in the relationship between subjective time and the on-
slaught of history that characterized this "age under construction."[23] His works
continually try to reconcile "the passing moment and . . . all the suggestions of
eternity that it contains;"[24] his malaise stemmed from his inability to accept an
urban landscape whose realities were as literal and impermanent as those depicted, for example, in Auguste Bertsch's 1855 sequential snapshots of traffic
streaming through the gates of the city, the "Passage de la Barrière Blanche"
(figs. 1.[10], 1.[11]). As Susan Buck-Morss has aptly pointed out, Paris is not often
described in Baudelaire's poems; it enters into his oeuvre not as a concrete environment, a precisely described mise-en-scène, but rather as a "disconnected sequence of optical displays," image bites setting the stage for "those moments of
existence that Baudelaire did not so much experience as endure."[25] The psychic
splintering, the constant movement of fantasy and desire discussed so brilliantly
in Leo Bersani's book *Baudelaire and Freud,*[26] fractured any global vision of
Paris this flaneur could perceive. Like the flickering scenes in early cinema, his
city kept moving in and out of focus.

The famous poem "The Swan,"[27] for instance, constantly moves between the poet's actual physical experience of the new Place du Carrousel, his
memories of events that once occurred in the old Place, and his mythical musings
about Andromache and other sufferers. Literal experience serves only as a
springboard for his fantasies and nightmares. His subjective pain continually
vacillates between the personal and the more general; his sadness is the swan's,

fig 1.[10]

A. Bertsch, *Passage de la Barrière Blanche,* 1855
(Société Française de la Photographie, Paris)

fig 1.[11]

A. Bertsch, *Passage de la Barrière Blanche #2,* 1855
(Société Française de la Photographie)

escaped from the poultry market and unable to find a lake, but it is also the pain of Greek mythology, exiles from Africa, and prisoners everywhere. The specific transforms itself, by virtue of its magnitude, into the global: Paris itself, and the upheavals it suffers, become by extension allegories of pain that reverberate through time and space.

The narrator himself, in this context, is transformed into an allegory: a human counterpart to the Tour Saint Jacques, he is an exile-in-time, imprisoned in a temporal space out of sync with his soul. As shifting and unstable as the monuments in the city, this man's historical identity was seriously undermined in a world of constant traffic and unremitting progress. Which brings us back, unavoidably, to Le Secq's photographic catastrophe, the *Album Berger.* Included in this album is a photograph of the old Place du Carrousel *(fig. 1.⁸),* not yet the one Baudelaire would see and Baldus would photograph in 1860 *(fig. 1.⁹)* but still, by 1852, marked by the demolition of the old stables of the king. This is a strange image, almost lunar, somewhat blurred. The Tuileries, not yet connected to the Louvre as they would be in the mid-1850s, define the limits of deep space, set off by the Arc du Carrousel. But in spite of the orderly geometries of the space, the whole foreground of the image is, literally, littered with the debris of destruction and ruin. There is no swan here, castigating God for its enslavement and deprivation; Andromache is nowhere in evidence. There are only the traces of reality, riddled with loss—the desolation of "those who lose what can never be found / again." [28]

And this irretrievable loss plays itself out in *time,* which transforms a city into a chasm of change, as deep a black hole as the pit in the foreground of this image that serves, ultimately, to separate Le Secq from his previous experience of Paris. Leo Bersani has speculated that the Realist writers, coming of age during the same *époque,* described the world so minutely in order to transfer their own emotional beings into the objects around them: "What we discover in much 19th century fiction is indeed a mirror, but it is displaced: instead of the artist's work having become a mirror of the world, it is the world which the artist has transformed into a mirror. The willed separation of the author from the world he describes has the effect of immobilizing the author's self in allego-rized social history. . . . Affectivity is, so to speak, relocated in a world cluttered with things which the writer has to describe in order to *see* his own existence."[29]

Viewed in the context of the shifting times and spaces of nineteenth-century Paris, Bersani's words can be seen as a definition of the plight of photog-raphers whose "willed separation" from experience was perhaps an inevitable consequence of historical upheaval. Not yet as fixated on the art/subjectivity connotations that would be the hallmark of modern photographic aesthetics after Peter Henry Emerson and Alfred Stieglitz, nineteenth-century image mak-ers appear to us more objective than their twentieth-century counterparts; their images seem almost cold when viewed by contemporary standards, as if their authors, like the Realist writers, were trying to be transparent, to disappear. But maybe that is because, as Bersani said, they are trying to find themselves in a displaced mirror. Maybe the world they expected to see was, more intimately than now, the world of their affectivity; maybe the objects they viewed, the spaces they walked through, the cities they lived in seemed, until Haussmann's irreparable debacle, to define more completely who they were.

In that case, the photos of Le Secq show us, with astonishing clarity, the rupture in time that would cause the broken identities, so obvious in Baudelaire's poetry and Edouard Manet's painting, that we call modernism. In the *Album Berger,* the particularities of history bear witness simultaneously to physical space and those "memories [that] weigh more than stone."[30] Like Daguerre, Le Secq is showing us a time frame parallel to his own experience, even though his image might have transcribed the exact details of the sight before his eyes. A temporal exile like Baudelaire, he is making manifest his alienation, his inability to enjoy a direct and unmediated relationship to his environment: his eyes' in-ability to find the reflection in the mirror of his mind. His Paris, uprooted in time, can no longer be, in any stable sense, a place: a nonspace, like the passing visions seen from a train, it can only be seen through a temporal glass, darkly.

This disjunction of sense and sensibility is seminal to all the chapters in this book. It links the limitless expanses of the train tracks to the time travel inherent in Nadar's forays into the catacombs, it connects the search for the void in hot air balloons to the frantic pace of the crowds on Haussmann's new streets, it links the macrocosm of a panoramic painting to the microcosm of a snapshot, and the fleeting moments of a stereograph to the interminable regard of a daguerreotype. Paris here is like the center of a vortex, radiating outward as the hub of new transportation and image networks even as it implodes inward in the misery of individual souls buffeted by the winds of change. And these Parisian views, trapped in their historical moment yet struggling often to either define, overcome, arrest, or transcend it, become like the looking glass onto another world whose inhabitants, like us, were voyagers struggling to traverse the barriers of time.

II

Parisian Views

T he following is an essay about vision, a series of speculations about the changes in perception that accompany the
changes in a society's visual space. The essay itself is a Parisian
view, a look across time at a Paris in the process of transforming
itself, destroying its old material and spiritual form and creating
one that, for better or worse, was a reflection of the Industrial Age.
As the physical structure of the city disappeared—as its buildings,
shops, neighborhoods, and interlocking social relations were
obliterated and new ones took shape—Parisians' images of the
city—their habits, interactions, memories, and perceptions—underwent drastic and often discomforting metamorphoses. It is in
their discomfort, and in the shifting images and patterns of the
Paris of the Second Empire, that we in the twentieth century can
view ourselves, can witness the psychological, spiritual, and physical birth pangs of an urban image that was to become the foundation of our own. So this Parisian view is one that, though looking
backward, points forward toward the making of the contemporary world.

E y e s

Between 1855 and his death in 1867, Baudelaire composed a series of fifty prose poems. During his lifetime, some of these short pieces were published as feuilletons for the daily or weekly mass-circulation Parisian papers; after his death, the completed works were collected and published as *Paris Spleen* in 1868. These prose poems are among the great urban writings, growing out of a tradition including Villon, Diderot, Balzac, Hugo, and Eugène Sue and yet drastically altering the traditional terms of their discussion of the city. For Baudelaire's prose poems, in both form and content, were the first literary works to be inspired by the modern urban environment. Even as Baudelaire composed the pieces in *Paris Spleen,* Georges-Eugène Haussmann, working under the authority of Emperor Napoleon III, was systematically demolishing the medieval Paris of Baudelaire's youth and building in its place the city of today. The prose poems are about this process—about the dramas of the death and rebirth of a city, and the traumatic upheavals such profound physical changes create in the souls of those who live through them.

One of the most poignant, and one of the latest, of these short pieces was "The Eyes of the Poor," written in 1864. It chronicles an encounter between two lovers, and between these lovers and a poor family. As a basis for a discussion of the changing social—and visual—relations in Haussmann's Paris, the piece is worth quoting in full:

Ah! So you would like to know why I hate you today? It will certainly be harder for you to understand than for me to explain, for you are, I believe, the most perfect example of feminine impermeability that exists.

We had spent a long day together which to me had seemed short. We had duly promised each other that all our thoughts should be shared in common, and that our two souls henceforth should be but one—a dream which, after all, has nothing original about it except that, although dreamed by every man on earth, it has been realized by none.

That evening, a little tired, you wanted to sit down in front of a new café forming the corner of a new boulevard still littered with rubbish but that already displayed proudly its unfinished splendors. The café was dazzling. Even the gas burned with all the ardor of a debut, and lighted with all its might the blinding whiteness of the walls, the expanse of mirrors, the gold cornices and moldings, fat-cheeked pages dragged along by hounds on leash, laughing ladies with falcons on their wrists, nymphs and goddesses bearing on their heads piles of fruits, patés and game, Hebes and Ganymedes holding out little amphoras of syrups or parti-colored ices: all history and all mythology pandering to gluttony.

On the street directly in front of us, a worthy man of about forty, with tired face and greying beard, was standing holding a small boy by the hand and carrying on his arm another little thing, still too weak to walk. He was playing nurse-maid, taking the children for an evening stroll. They were in rags. The three faces were extraordinarily serious, and those six eyes stared fixedly at the new café with admiration, equal in degree but differing in kind according to their ages.

The eyes of the father said: "How beautiful it is! How beautiful it is! All the gold of the poor world must have found its way onto those walls!" The eyes of the little boy: "How beautiful it is! How beautiful it is! But it is a house where only people who are not like us can go." As for the baby, he was much too fascinated to express anything but joy—utterly stupid and profound.

Song writers say that pleasure ennobles the soul and softens the heart. The song was right that evening as far as I was concerned. Not only was I touched by this family of eyes, but I was even a little ashamed of our glasses and decanters, too big for our thirst. I turned my eyes to look into yours, dear love, to read my thoughts in them; and as I plunged my eyes into your eyes, so beautiful and so curiously soft, into those green eyes, home of Caprice and governed by the Moon, you said: "Those

*people are insufferable with their great saucer eyes. Can't you tell the pro-
prietor to send them away?"*

*So you see how difficult it is to understand one another, my dear
angel, how incommunicable thought is, even between two people in love.*[1]

This is a poem about change: about shifting emotional and social dramas acted out within the context of a city in transition, in a café whose showy
splendor rises from the contrasting rubble of a town in ruins. The situation is
perceived from only one person's point of view, but that point of view encom-
passes a far broader range of experiences and interactions than would have been
possible even ten years before. Haussmann's rebuilding of Paris aimed, first and
foremost, at eliminating congestion in the center city and freely promoting the
circulation of traffic to all parts of Paris. To this end, Haussmann, Napoleon
III's prefect of the Seine, "pierced" (his word)[2] streets through the crowded heart
of the old city, in the process demolishing the homes, shops, studios, meeting
places, and settled lives of countless inhabitants. These old Parisian neighborhoods, overcrowded and unsanitary, had grown up haphazardly from the time
of the Middle Ages; narrow streets, short and winding, with buildings blocking
the way at every turn, discouraged movement through the city, and in *L'As-
somoir,* set in the 1850s, Zola could describe the lives of denizens who rarely,
in a lifetime, traveled more than a few blocks from home. With the wholesale
destruction of these tightly packed neighborhoods and the creation of large boulevards throughout the city, Haussmann, as Marshall Berman wrote, "opened
up the whole of the city, for the first time in its history, to all its inhabitants.
Now, at last, it was possible to move not only within neighborhoods, but
through them. Now, after centuries of life as a cluster of isolated cells, Paris was
becoming a unified physical and human space."[3]

Yet in unifying these "isolated cells" and making possible the free flow
of their inhabitants, Haussmann permanently altered the interactions possible
for city residents. One of his first priorities had been to cut through and destroy
the unhealthy, unsightly, and economically underprivileged areas that had been

growing wildly and, in their horrific overpopulation, overtaking the heart of the town.[4] By so doing, the prefect hoped to roust the poor (who posed, he felt, a threat to both the city's health and the stability of its government) to the outlying *banlieues*. But in opening up circulation in Paris, Haussmann also opened up the whole of the city to the poor—who for the first time became visible on the streets and boulevards, constant reminders of the squalor that lurked behind the wealth of the dazzling cafés and shops designed for the bourgeoisie. The narrator's confrontation with the "eyes of the poor," the central incident in this prose parable, was made possible by Haussmann's *grands travaux*.

These great works also served to change the face of love in the big city. The narrator and his girlfriend are involved in a love affair that unfolds in the context of the crowded and glittering urban streets. They also are not "isolated cells" but people whose emotional bonds are forged and broken within the political, social, economic, and physical structures that provide the backdrop for their interaction. This modern, urban environment allows these two people to spend an enchanted day wrapped up in each other, alone in a crowd and yet enjoying the beauties and amusements the city has to offer—but it also, inescapably and unavoidably, intrudes on their relationship, forcing their private love into a public domain that would not have existed for them a decade before. They, like the café, are part of the street's irresistible spectacle, an amorous display for the passerby whose presence helps to ignite the sparks of their passion. But the streets, in turn, by compelling them to face the contrast between their own privilege and the deprivations of others, have forced them to grapple with the larger context of their emotional life and to see each other in the harsh light of the city's economic realities. Their love, as Baudelaire realizes, is no longer solely their own; this private emotion, in the course of the poem, becomes part of a social fabric larger than the individuals involved and slips out of their control.

"The Eyes of the Poor" is essentially about an emotional movement: a shift from love to hate, from fantasy to reality, from closeness to alienation. The narrator sees his lover within the context of her politics and realizes through this "how difficult it is to understand one another . . . , how incommunicable thought is, even between two people in love." The urban environment has provided the backdrop for the fantasies of their affair, and at the same time it has provided the circumstances that prove its limitations. Love has encountered the social world—and it has been vanquished.

Yet this emotional drama is enacted not through events or actions or even dialogue but through the interactions of *eyes*. The prose poem describes, in great detail, what the narrator "sees" both in terms of his literal and his perceptive vision; and his readings of the four other people present are based solely on his sensitivity to their eyes. The eyes of the poor, the father and his two children, reflect three different responses to the splendor of the café: the father's admiration and bitterness for "all the gold of the poor world," the eldest child's admiration and his understanding that such places are not for "people . . . like us," and the baby's "joy—utterly stupid and profound." Seeing these reactions, and feeling himself touched by the "family of eyes" that allows people to penetrate deeply into each others' souls, the narrator "plunges" his eyes into the "beautiful and so curiously soft" eyes of his lover, assuming he will "read (his) thoughts in them." And yet, with the one line of dialogue in the entire poem, his girlfriend completely destroys his fantasies—about her, about their relationship, and about the "family of eyes" that, by providing windows onto each others' souls, might give human beings access to the profoundest thoughts of others.

The sociologist Georg Simmel has remarked that "Interpersonal relationships in big cities are distinguished by a marked preponderance of the activity of the eye over the activity of the ear. The main reason for this is the public means of transportation. Before the development of buses, railroads and trams in the nineteenth century, people had never been in a position of having to look at one another for long minutes or even hours without speaking to each other."[5]

This new form of purely visual social interaction created a peculiar and very modern form of uneasiness, which was mitigated in part by the "physiologies," small paperbacks that were the most popular form of literature in Paris in the first half of the nineteenth century. These books were easy-to-understand, trivialized versions of the scientific physiognomies written by Johann Kaspar

Lavater and Ferdinand von Gall in the eighteenth century, and they benignly described the various types of people that one might encounter on the city streets. By making it clear that everyone could be read and assessed by virtue of their physical characteristics, the physiologies, in Walter Benjamin's words, "assured people that everyone was, unencumbered by any factual knowledge, able to make out the profession, the character, the background, and the life-style of passers-by. . . . If that sort of thing could be done, then, to be sure, life in the big city was not nearly so disquieting as it probably seemed to people." [6]

Yet in "The Eyes of the Poor," Baudelaire's narrator discovers that life in the new social world, the world of Haussmann's Paris, is not so simple and clear-cut: one can never be sure of one's readings of one's intimates, let alone of strangers. One may "see" more people in Haussmann's Paris—but in spite of the increased circulation, people are still "isolated cells." Five pairs of eyes "talk" in this prose poem; but since they are all registering different responses to the same situation, these eyes are babbling in tongues. We see only through the eyes of the narrator, but throughout the course of the poem his vision alters radically. At first he sees a world united by the "family of eyes," and carried away by the prose, we accept his interpretation of people, places, and events. But as soon as his girlfriend speaks, the picture changes—and all of his perceptions are called into question. What we are left with is a scene of multiple and shifting perspectives: of viewpoints as unstable as a city that disappears and is rebuilt, and as isolated as the eye of a man or a woman behind a camera. For Baudelaire's writing reflects the turmoil of an era, the era that gave us not only Haussmann's *grands travaux* but also the legacy of a socially functional photography. The modern urban environment and the modern image-form came of age hand-in-hand on the streets of Baudelaire's Paris during the Second Empire.

Vistas

In Baudelaire's narrator, we see the individual struggling to come to terms with himself — and others — within a rapidly changing social world. We witness events, interactions, and emotions from the point of view of one person, a person whose perceptual possibilities, as mentioned earlier, were being vastly enriched by the newly created street life in Haussmann's Paris. This individual voyeur reached archetypal proportions in the person of the flaneur: the solitary stroller, meandering through the crowd, who was to become such a staple in nineteenth-century French art and literature. This dawdling people watcher, the prototype of the contemporary street photographer, was in his heyday during the Second Empire, and Haussmann's reconstruction of the city was a major reason for his ascendancy. The prefect's demolition of the impacted old *quartiers;* his building of scenic boulevards lined with sidewalks that made promenades both possible and fashionable; his encouragement of local businesses built on the new streets; and his installation of 15,000 gaslights that stimulated nocturnal strolling by making it safer and allowing shops to remain open until 10:00 P.M.: all contributed to the formation of the street life for which Paris is today famous.[7]

Haussmann's Paris was, above all, a bourgeois and capitalistic city, dedicated to ostentation, consumption, and display. Shops and cafés sprang up on the new boulevards; shopping arcades and then, during the 1860s, the first department stores (like Bon Marché) provided centers of both pleasure and commerce where those lucky enough to profit from investments, speculations, or job opportunities created by the rebuilding could spend their money; and the Universal Expositions (*Expositions Universelles,* the nineteenth-century's version of world's fairs) held in Paris in 1855 and 1867 *(fig. 2.¹)* encouraged the mingling of merchandise and men from diverse nations. As Walter Benjamin has pointed out, the Paris of the Second Empire marks the emergence of the commodity culture—a culture in which the display of goods was surpassed only by the display of the people in the street who came to look at them and at each other.[8] By encouraging this circulation of the crowd, Haussmann's Paris opened up new images and interactions, and guaranteed that the boulevards would become the focal point of Parisian life.

The boulevards were also the core of Napoleon III's urban plan, which was conceived and carried out during the miraculously short span of seventeen years between 1853 and 1869. The story, told by Haussmann in his *Mémoires* and repeated countless times since, is that the day the prefect of the Seine took office, the emperor presented him with a map of Paris, upon which were marked all of the streets that he proposed to build.[9] Haussmann goes to great lengths to give his emperor the credit for originating the idea and the general plan for the

fig 2.[1]

Bisson Brothers, (Louis-Auguste, Auguste-Rosalie), 1867, *Universal Exposition, Hall of Exhibitions* (Bibliothèque Nationale, Paris)

transformation of Paris. Yet it was the prefect who carried out these plans and who, in the process, conceptualized and realized what Sigfried Giedion has called "the metropolis of the industrial era." [10]

Haussmann was faced with a massive, and unprecedented, task. As David Pinkney points out: "Parts of cities, even entire new cities like Versailles, Karlsruhe or Saint-Petersburg, had been planned and built, but no one before had attempted to refashion an entire old city." [11] The prefect faced technical problems that had never before been an issue; for instance, when he took office there was no accurate survey map of Paris, and one had to be made before he could even begin the transformation process. Such a mundane but critical example points up the most modern aspect of Haussmann's accomplishment: no one before him had considered the city as a single organism, a unit that could be conceptualized, planned as a unified system, and realized through technical, scientific, and mechanical means. Urban planning, *urbanisme* in French, did not yet exist. As Françoise Choay points out in *Histoire de la France Urbaine: La Ville de l'Age Industriel:* "The birth of urbanism is dated 1867, the year when the monumental work of the Spanish engineer Ildefonso Cerda, the *General Theory of Urbanization* which gave the discipline its name, appeared in Madrid." [12] Yet over a decade before that, Haussmann was realizing, in practice rather than in theory, the same general principles in his restructuring of the capital of France.

The boulevards that were the lifeblood of this new urban organism were, as Marshall Berman put it, "arteries in an urban circulatory system." [13] The wide (up to 100 yards across) streets built by the prefect were designed to allow traffic to flow through the center of the city and move easily, in a straight line, from end to end; to link the railroad stations to the rest of the city and the heart of Paris to the outlying areas; to clear the slums and thus eliminate a health and crime hazard; to open up tree-lined, light-filled vistas, punctuated by green *places* and squares that could provide health-enhancing breathing space to city inhabitants; and to make it possible for troops to travel quickly throughout the city and impossible for revolutionary barricades to be erected. Complemented by the systems of parks, of sewers, and of water supply constructed during the same period, these boulevards transformed the old Paris, a city of individual buildings, monuments, and neighborhoods, into a vast and unified urban network—one that became regional in scope after the outlying suburbs were annexed in 1859.

Thus the same boulevards that had one meaning for an individual like Baudelaire had quite another when viewed from the perspective of Haussmann's urban plan. Like the love of Baudelaire's narrator, the streets had two faces that coexisted in an uneasy tension, a tension that could, with a slight shift in point of view, turn into a contradiction. The boulevards that so vastly enriched the individual experience of the numerous flaneurs of Paris were, at the same time, the structural underpinnings of a city that, by rejecting human scale in favor of a larger conceptual scheme, began to threaten both the primacy and the independence of the individual. In creating their networks of boulevards, Napoleon III and Haussmann thought only peripherally about the comfort and welfare of the people who were to live on them. One example: residential apartments were built exclusively by private companies and speculators, and although Haussmann dictated their outward appearance in conformity with the aesthetic effect he wished to create, there were few regulations about the insides, and he ignored the fact that many buildings with fine exteriors had slumlike interiors.[14] In other words, city residents were, more and more, forced to come to terms with physical spaces created in response to other, more abstract exigencies and conceived in relation to large-scale technical or economic questions rather than in relation to human beings.

Haussmann's systemic approach to the city, for instance, demanded not only the demolition of buildings but also the suppression of local color in both the neighborhoods and the terrain of Paris. In piercing through the old *quartiers,* the prefect destroyed not only medieval buildings but also diverse ways of life and work,[15] and he replaced the multiplicity of classes and lifestyles with a homogeneous and bourgeois order, both economic and physical. Definitely a man of his time, Haussmann had a passion for geometry, uniformity, and measurement that causes contemporary historians like Françoise Choay to term his programs "the urbanism of regularization." [16] Short, narrow, winding, and picturesque old streets were replaced by straight roads leading off into the distance farther than the eye could see and lending an air of regularity to everything. The accurate survey map mentioned earlier was necessary because Haussmann demanded that his new boulevards be not only absolutely straight but also absolutely level; in numerous instances, for example the present Avenue Victor Hugo, hilly ground was significantly lowered and leveled to better fit into his visual plan. [17] The circular or rectangular *places,* conceived to offer light and air and greenery in the midst of traffic, serve as points of exchange between streets that often intersect on the diagonal. The more points of exchange, the better Haussmann liked it, and the prefect was fetishistic about the *places'* symmetry; on the Place de l'Etoile, for instance, he assured it by creating uniformly shaped building lots between every pair of radiating streets and decreeing exactly the way the buildings upon them could be constructed. [18]

Such an imposition not only changed the face of the city but also dictated the ways in which people could live within it—and Parisians had much to say, both pro and con, about the "urbanism of regularization" during the years of Haussmann's administration. While city denizens seemed aware that something had to be done about the capital, agreeing with Maxine Du Camp that "after 1848, Paris was about to become uninhabitable," there was much controversy about Haussmann's ultimate achievement. [19] Vociferously heard among the prefect's critics were those who felt that he had created the "neutered city of civilized people." [20] His "straight line," they said, "has killed the picturesque, the unexpected. The Rue de Rivoli is a symbol; a new street, long, wide, cold, frequented by men as well dressed, affected and cold as the street itself. . . . The street existed only in Paris, and the street is dying." [21] One of the most amusing comments, however, is from *Maison Neuve,* a play put on by Victorien Sardou in 1866, in which an older man argues with his niece and nephew about the new Paris. He ends his speech by saying: "(I) beg leave to think it fortunate that God himself was ignorant of this marvelous municipal system, and did not choose to arrange the trees in the forest in rows . . . with all the stars above in two straight lines." [22]

Haussmann's passion for straight lines was part of an aesthetic that, though neoclassical in conception, was significantly different by virtue of its scale and its aims. One of old Paris's problems, as the prefect saw it, was that too often the old and venerated monuments—the churches, the state buildings, the columns, and statues—had become so enmeshed in the dense and overpopulated fabric of the city that they were almost invisible. Among his first priorities was the disengagement of these monuments—the demolition of all that stood in their way—and the creation of vistas that could set these prized jewels in their proper perspective. His boulevards were constructed to provide just these perspectives. Whenever possible he built streets that terminated in a preexisting monument; when that was not possible, he built a church or a new monument that could serve as the culmination point of a promenade down one of his paved roads. [23] His boulevards, therefore, were conceived as Parisian views; his shaping of the visual space of the urban environment was goal and object oriented. The trees lining the boulevards, the uniform buildings that faced the streets, and the straight lines of the roads themselves: all of these were designed to enhance the vistas so central to Haussmann's planning of Paris, the vistas that were supposed to channel the vision of the promeneur as effectively as the lens of a camera.

And yet this neoclassical insistence on streets terminating in monumental vistas begins to break down in Haussmann's Paris, for no longer was the prefect working with short streets that could be taken in at a glance by the pedestrian. The older model of the city had been built to human scale, a scale that was transcended in the new Paris of the Industrial Age. This new city was regional in conception, and its structure was based on what Sigfried Giedion calls "the cannonshot boulevard, seemingly without end." [24] Some of his streets (like the Rue de Rivoli) are three miles long—a length that can be conceptualized but not readily perceived by the senses. So his vistas were often lost by a promeneur, who perceived as his point of reference only the endless street. The aesthetic order that Haussmann imposed on his capital, therefore, could only be grasped on a map, or by a visual overview (which makes panoramic and aerial photographs particularly relevant to this period). In his systemic planning of the city, in his insistence on a scale and range beyond human sense perceptions, Haussmann began, therefore, in spite of his fetish for monuments and vistas, to destroy the primacy of objects. In his Paris, the street—the means of transport, the channel of relationship between objects—becomes dominant.

This can be seen more clearly in Haussmann's nonmonumental architecture. The prefect found early on that architects, trained to design single structures for specific sites, were of little use to him in his planning of Paris. His was a city built by technicians and engineers, men like Adolphe Alphand, Eugène Belgrand, and M. Descamps, who were committed to working with mechanical means and perceiving problems on a larger scale.[25] Most of the buildings lining the boulevards were built by private companies and real estate speculators; and yet these companies were bound by imperial decrees that insisted on a uniformity of construction. Napoleon III's and Haussmann's insistence on uniformity lies within the tradition of classical city planning. But on such a large scale, and in the context of these "cannonshot boulevards," the repetition of forms served to create a sweeping rhythm that negated the unique self-containment of individual structures and instead emphasized and enhanced the visual dynamism of the street itself.

Such a shift—from a point of view that focused on objects to one that emphasizes instead the relations between them—completely altered the human experience of the urban environment. The city had once been a physical structure based on units—people, buildings, neighborhoods; it was now a place in which these units were subsumed into a broader relational context whose range far exceeded that of its inhabitants. And the street that had once served as simply a link between stable buildings and *quartiers* had suddenly burst into motion— had become not only the means of circulation but the end. In this context, the boulevards that provided enriched experience for the individual also called into question not only one's primacy but also the primacy and stability of all of one's reference points. The streets that were the stomping ground of the flaneur simultaneously began to threaten him with negation, for in them the point of view of the promeneur was superseded by the larger, extra-human systemic overview. Those who lived through the transformation of Paris were, therefore, living through an era of multiple and shifting perspectives, a time when the confrontation between human experience and the artificial range of large-scale visual spaces was causing vistas to break down, objects to lose their solidity, and people to redefine not only their habits and lifestyles but also their very perceptions of their physical selves within the environment. In Haussmann's Paris, everything was in motion — except, of course, photography.

Views

In this context, a photograph — especially one produced with the long exposure times necessary in the early years of the medium's history — seems like a still point in a turning world. In some ways, photographs did function as a means to stop time — a time that, during the Second Empire, seemed to be moving too fast. But in other ways, photography itself was part of the movement and change, seminal to forging the new sense perceptions and defining the new visual spaces that mark this period in Parisian history. Photography was simultaneously the apotheosis of individual, subjective vision and the systematization of vision within a larger, intra-individual cultural context; it was both a tool to reflect the particular "eyes" of Baudelaire's narrator and a mechanical means of mass communication that, like Haussmann's circulatory scheme, forced subjective vision out of the realm of the idiosyncratic and personal and into the realm of the social. As such it embodies within itself the paradoxes, and the multiple perspectives, inherent in life during the Second Empire.

Photography came of age as a socially functional medium of representation in Paris during the years of Haussmann's administration, so the early accomplishments of the medium must be seen as inextricably intertwined with the equally revolutionary birth of the modern urban environment. The same historical period that gave us the city of the industrial age also gave us the means to efficiently and cheaply reproduce and disseminate permanently fixed photographic prints. While Daguerre's announcement of his daguerreotype process had startled the world and officially initiated the photographic age, certain technical advances in Paris in the early 1850s served to transform photography from a limited, personal image-making form into a socially viable one. Daguerre's process, until then in vogue, had yielded only a single direct positive on a metal plate; Louis-Désiré Blanquart-Evrard's newly perfected process, based on the calotype of Fox Talbot and perhaps also on improvements by David Octavius Hill and Robert Adamson, made it possible for multiple prints to be made (and permanently fixed) on paper from a single paper negative.[26] And men like Blanquart-Evrard, in choosing to exploit the industrial possibilities of this advance, laid the groundwork for the image systems that circulated photographic prints to the public just as Haussmann's plan of Paris circulated traffic.

Blanquart-Evrard, referred to by Isabelle Jammes as "the Gutenberg of photography,"[27] was born in Lille in 1802, and studied chemistry and painted miniatures on ivory and porcelain before turning to photography in the 1840s. Between 1847 and 1851, he succeeded in creating rich, permanent prints that were not subject to fading—a major stumbling block both in the production and the commercial viability of photography until that time. His process involved the use of albumen, which worked to adhere the silver salts to the surface of paper; the washing of prints in pure water; and the application of gold salts as a toning agent: not new inventions, but new uses of older methods intelligently applied. From his earliest involvement with the medium, Blanquart-Evrard had pushed for its industrialization, and by 1849 he had figured out ways to make glass negatives from paper ones for this purpose. In 1851 he opened the doors of his *imprimerie* at Lille, which in the five years of its existence printed 100,000 negatives for commercial purposes.

fig 2.²

Maxime Du Camp, *Les Deux Speos, Ibsamboul*, 1850
(Bibliothèque Nationale, Paris)

Three types of activities went on at Lille. Negatives were printed there, for a fee, for artists, publishers, and amateurs. Albums of photographs were produced by the *imprimerie* itself, and the plates for larger, more elaborate book works, edited by Gide and Baudry, were made under Blanquart-Evrard's direction. This was the first successful commercial photographic printing business (Talbot had failed in England in the 1840s), and its impressive list of published books and albums includes, besides the famous *Egypte, Nubie, Palestine et Syrie* by Maxime Du Camp *(fig. 2.²)*, editions documenting religious art, contemporary art, Belgium, Brussels, and the monuments of Paris.

Blanquart-Evrard had rivals in the photographic publishing business by 1851, when Eugene Piot produced a portfolio entitled *L'Italie Monumentale* (which actually appeared *before* the publication of Du Camp's book). Other competitors were active by 1853–1854, including H. de Fonteny, who produced Teynard's *Egypte et Nubie, sites et monuments les plus interessants pour l'étude de l'art et l'histoire,* and the lithographic printer Joseph Lemercier, who in preparing the prints for Charles Blanc's *L'Oeuvre de Rembrandt reproduit par la photographie* essentially created the first photographically illustrated art history book.

The importance of such editions should not be underestimated for they made photographs widely accessible to a broad public—and Blanquart-Evrard made considerable efforts during the five years of his *imprimerie's* existence to lower prices in order to make the works even more commercially viable. The subject matter of these books and albums is relevant as well, for in their emphasis on foreign countries and exotic landscapes and art they reflect an important preoccupation of the Second Empire. These were the years when France, catching up to other European countries, constructed its new railroads and expanded its maritime fleet. The speed of messages began to exceed the speed of physical travel when telegraphic apparatus began operating at the bourse in 1852. Internal expansionism was matched by a change in foreign policy: Napoleon III aggressively involved France in various escapades in countries as far flung as the Crimea and Mexico.[28] The preoccupation with travel, which could only be undertaken by the privileged few, was satisfied for many by the distribution of photographic imagery, which therefore played a great role in expanding the sensory perceptions and global knowledge of the populace. Suddenly architectural monuments, views of foreign cities, documentary records of exotic landscapes, and art objects *(fig. 2.³)* from numerous countries—physically inaccessible to the average person—became, through photography, part of the cultural image-bank and filtered directly into the mainstream of Western society.

Photography's ability to telescope space—to bring objects and places closer to people by way of reproduction—was intimately related to its ability to confound time: to freeze a moment, to bring the past into the present, and transform the present into history. Photography's relationship to time was brought into the foreground of public consciousness after Frederick Scott Archer's 1851 introduction of the wet collodion process, which shortened exposure times and became widely used in France and elsewhere for portraiture and outdoor work,

fig 2.[3]
Artist unknown, L.-D. Blanquart-Evrard (editor), reproduction of Rubens's
Henri IV receiving the portrait of Marie de Medici,
from *Mélanges Photographiques,* 1851–1853
(Bibliothèque Nationale, Paris)

including street photographs. The Second Empire was also the period during which Disdéri, who took out a patent for cartes-de-visite photographs in Paris in 1854, succeeded in developing a time and labor efficient business for the cheap mass production of portraits.[29] As Max Kozloff wrote in his article "Nadar and the Republic of Mind":

People (of the Second Empire) rendered homage to a then grand ideal — Progress. A marvelous index of progress was speed, the increased rapidity with which things could get done, and space could be traversed. One has only to look at that great public castle or temple, the nineteenth-century railroad station, to see how arrivals and departures — mass movement in short — were glorified. And wasn't the photograph itself a characteristic witness of the age's lust for accelerated record and communication, power and efficiency? What once took weeks or months to limn by hand could now be accomplished in minutes, mechanically. So urgent was the need for progress that photographic exposures were reduced to seconds. Time, in 1860, was burning up.[30]

Speed and the telescoping of time and space were dominant characteristics of this new, mechanical, visual medium — just as they were central to the new Paris, which was designed by Napoleon III and Haussmann with the rapid traversing of time and space in mind. Just as photography brought the large, physically inaccessible world closer spatially by reproduction, Haussmann's broad boulevards pierced through the city and connected disparate parts of Paris that until then had been separated by a chaotic mass of medieval streets. But there are other points of similarity as well. Walter Benjamin, in his essay "The Work of Art in the Age of Mechanical Reproduction," describes how photography destroys the "aura" of a work of art, or even a landscape, by undermining the physical presence, duration, and authenticity of objects and substituting a plurality of copies for a unique original.[31] Books like Du Camp's *Egypte, Nubie, Palestine et Syrie* and Blanc's *L'Oeuvre de Rembrandt reproduit par la photo-*

graphie, and widely disseminated single images of objects, landscapes, cities, and even persons began, during the Second Empire, to destroy the primacy of physical objects just as surely as did Haussmann's circulatory scheme. By increasing circulation—in one case of traffic, in the other of reproductions—both the new Paris and the new visual medium vastly expanded individual perceptual capabilities while simultaneously undermining the physical bases of sensory experience.

Given this spiritual kinship, it is not surprising that, from the first, photography was involved in Napoleon III's administration and that it played a significant role in the Haussmannization of the city. Like the technicians and engineers who accomplished the rebuilding of Paris, photographers were, by definition, modern men working with mechanical means, and during the years of the Second Empire the lines between artists, amateurs, and commercial photographers had not yet been clearly drawn. As a consequence, many who were known as major photographic artists during these years, like Henri Le Secq and Gustave Le Gray, also did major work on commission for the government. And a number of the photographers who were attracted to documenting Paris—sometimes on their own initiative, sometimes for a speculative market, and sometimes on assignment—were trained as, and often continued to be, Salon painters, interested in exploring and expanding the possibilities of a new medium of representation.

Several critics and historians, most notably Walter Benjamin in "A Short History of Photography"[32] and Gisèle Freund in *Photography and Society,*[33] have remarked on the quality of photographic work produced during the 1850s —a quality that, they feel, was lost when photography became heavily industrialized and commercialized in the 1860s. And while this point of view is well taken, it must be said that photography itself is a child of the Industrial Age, and only through its industrialization could it truly come into its own. Photography's relationship to Haussmannization represents one step in this complex process of maturation. As the various photographers worked to come to terms with the transformation of Paris, to shape a vision of both the old and the new environment that could orient them and their audience to a changing world, they forged remarkably diverse — and often conflicting — images of a city in transition, on its way to becoming the space of modernity.

The first project that must be mentioned in this respect had nothing to do with Haussmannization, or even the Second Empire, yet it set the stage for all subsequent architectural photography in France. This is the Mission Hélio-graphique, the first photographic survey of historical monuments in France, which was commissioned by the governmental Commission des Monuments Historiques (probably with the assistance of the newly established Société Hélio-graphique) in 1851, the year before Napoleon III announced the coup d'état that established the Second Empire. After examining portfolios, the Commission sent five men — Edouard-Denis Baldus, Hippolyte Bayard, Henri Le Secq, Gustave Le Gray and O. Mestral — to photograph in five different provincial centers of France. Though the mission faded out for mysterious reasons (most probably because at that time Blanquart-Evrard's process for making rich, permanent prints was not yet perfected), and only 300 paper negatives survive (along with very few prints; it seems that many of the negatives were never even printed and were simply stored away),[34] in commissioning the project the government, as Weston Naef has commented, "permitted some of France's most important pho-tographic artists to gain valuable field experience."[35]

Yet although the mission insured that France possessed the most experi-enced architectural photographers in the world, its aims must be emphasized. The mission's function was, essentially, conservative. The numerous negatives produced under its auspices were designed to preserve France's ancient *architec-tural heritage* — a heritage that was being threatened not only by industrializa-tion but also by restoration. The mission photographs, and the considerable number of images of ancient monuments extant from the period of the Second Empire (which now make up such a prized part of the photography collections in French and American art museums), must be seen in this context. These pho-tographs might have been produced by a modern mechanical medium on the cusp of the creation of the modern urban environment, but their primary function was to "preserve" the old structures and record the changes that had already occurred in the country's architectural patrimony. However revolutionary its invention might have been, photography became, during the Second Empire, the agent of visual and temporal preservation for a century that also invented hygienic and medical measures for the preservation of health, new methods for the conservation of food, and, of course, public museums for the conservation of art.[36]

Formally, one often sees the same disjunction—between radicalism of means and nostalgia of vision—in the pictures, the same reliance on old patterns of perception at a time when new patterns, recognized by artists as diverse as Baudelaire and, later, the impressionist painters, were being forged in the immediate environment every day. It must be emphasized, once again, that most of these early photographers were painters, trained in the Salon style, and their methods of constructing their pictures attest to these conservative ways of seeing. The series of views of Notre-Dame and the monuments of Paris, edited by Blanquart-Evrard in 1852 and 1853 and photographed by Le Secq, Fortier, Marville *(figs. 3.², 4.⁷)*, and some anonymous photographers, for instance, aims to showcase individual buildings and public sculptures, focusing on their physical form and architectural or ornamental detail. The environs, though pictorially well integrated, are incidental to the pictures that are primarily oriented toward specific and self-contained objects. Their emphasis on physical structures, at exactly the point in time when Haussmann was commencing the construction of a network of boulevards that would shatter the primacy of objects, is telling.

The confusions and ambiguities inherent in this type of photography were, however, inherent in Haussmann's urban planning as well. The conflicts between the prefect's tastes for the old and the new are evident even in the projected aims of his overall scheme for the city, and it is here that the parallels with this form of photography become striking. Just as Haussmann attempted, using thoroughly modern technical and conceptual means, to create neoclassical vistas, so many of the most important French photographers of the Second Empire used their new medium to create views based on older patterns of seeing that were rapidly becoming outmoded. And, just as Haussmann's systemic overview, with its cannonshot boulevards, ultimately undermined his monument-oriented vistas, so the new vision inherent in photography, with its foreshortenings, truncations, sensitivity to changes in form based on light and shadow, and ability to manipulate points of view, began to suggest new perceptual patterns that would undermine object-oriented ways of seeing.

A good example is Le Secq's *Flying Buttresses of the Cathedral, Reims, (fig. 2.⁴)* taken in 1852 and described by Weston Naef as "among the most advanced (compositions) of its time."[37] In choosing his point of view for this eccentric print that was to serve as a harbinger of things to come, Le Secq negated the ancient and venerable cathedral-as-object and focused instead on the details of its structural elements: the lines of force, the relational lines, which were the architectural network underlying the building's construction and which visually served to create a two-dimensional, abstract design of straight and curving lines, light and shadow. Such views became more common during the last quarter of the nineteenth century as more photographers began documenting the *grands travaux*. Most notable among the few photographers doing this type of work during the Second Empire were the partners in the little-known studio of Delmaet and Durandelle, active from 1860 to 1890, which specialized in documenting construction sites. In choosing points of view that eliminated context and focused instead on the structural skeletons of architectural works-in-progress, Delmaet and Durandelle created pictures that were both abstract and documentary, and that transformed metal beams, scaffolds, and pillars into forceful architectural anatomies celebrating the technical ingenuity of nineteenth-century engineers.[38]

The obscurity of these pictures, known mainly inside scholarly circles, contrasts sharply with the fame of many more nostalgic images by artists from Le Secq to Marville to Atget and points up, once again, the peculiar temporality that underlay the creation and perception of the built environment in nineteenth-century Paris—a built environment that in many ways suffered from the same time displacements that Baudelaire would characterize as "spleen" (see chap. 1).

fig 2.⁴
Henri Le Secq, *Flying Buttresses, Reims Cathedral,* 1852
(Bibliothèque Nationale, Paris)

fig 2.[5]
Delmaet and Durandelle Studio, *Construction of the Opera*, 1865–1872
(Bibliothèque Nationale, Paris)

The prefect's well-known emphasis on historicism—his seemingly arbitrary use, as Victor Hugo cynically commented (chap. 1), of diverse historical and national styles as architectural signifiers in new public buildings—was perhaps more than a simple negation or confusion of historical identity. It was also an attempt to create an empire in time as well as space—as Baudelaire described it in "The Eyes of the Poor," to have "all history and all mythology pander" to the glory of a public street theater in the making. For the grand boulevards were to encompass a temporal universality that could parallel the cultural universality evident in the new world's fairs and department stores.

This temporal bouillabaisse led, of course, to some strange contrasts and conflicts. By superimposing and juxtaposing historical styles, the prefect unleashed style from its moorings in meaning as surely as he unleashed the Tour St. Jacques from its community functions. The complex historical layers inherent in old European cities that have survived into the Industrial Age were in fact recreated in the architectural constructions of individual neighborhoods and even individual buildings—as can be seen when comparing Adolphe Braun's photograph of the finished Garnier Opéra building *(fig. 2.7)* with Delmaet and Durandelle Studio's pictures of the work-in-progress *(figs. 2.5, 2.6)*. The skeletal structure of this famous architectural wedding cake, criticized as "looking like a sideboard overloaded with knicknacks,"[39] is of course iron; but the construction crews politely covered its elegant network of metal beams with a lavish facade of sculpture, gilding, and varicolored stone. What you saw, in other words, was not necessarily what you got. And in the shifting centuries defined by these shifting points of view, we are back in the radiating time zones of Baudelaire's poetry and the Tour St. Jacques (see chap. 1).

This monument, like the city it served, was therefore a *site* that splintered into a series of *sights,* and its multiple perspectives sometimes yielded conflicting messages. In this respect the building itself was more than a setting for operatic theater. It was also a stage set reflecting and codifying what Mikhail Bakhtin would call the "chronotope" (literally "time-space") of nineteenth-century Parisian public street theater: the "metaphoric setting where historically

fig 2.[6]
Delmaet and Durandelle Studio, *Construction of the Opera*, 1865–1872
(Bibliothèque Nationale, Paris)

fig 2.[7]

Adolphe Braun, *The New Opera*, 1870s (Bibliothèque Nationale, Paris)

specific relations of power become visible and certain stories can take place."[40] Bakhtin's chronotope was always literary or artistic, but it seems fair to suggest that Haussmann's traumatic destruction and reconstruction of Paris opened up the possibility of seeing the city itself as a work of art, as a self-conscious metaphoric space responsive to the historical currents of an era. And just as "all history and all mythology" converged here, so did goods and people from all over the globe, transforming this city into a "cosmopolis, where the world (read European Empire) was every place co-present."[41]

This is an extremely important point, because it suggests that the time-space of Paris in the nineteenth century, encompassing as it did all history as well as all geography, was as much invisible as visible, as much distant as local,

fig 2.[8]

E. Baldus, *The Louvre, Imperial Library*, c. 1855
(Bibliothèque Nationale, Paris)

as much absent as present. This might be dubbed the era of empiricism, of positivism, of scientific and photographic documentation, but the theoretical emphasis on the physical universe took place at just the moment when the experience of this cosmopolis was in fact becoming less and less concrete. Even the physical environments of modern Paris, its street plans and monuments, cafés and stores, were increasingly shaped by the exigencies of larger, multinational social forces. Haussmann's historical architecture only masked the determinant influence of trains and travel, international capital and trade, military maneuvers, colonization, and global communications. As Rob Shields has so aptly commented, even the infrastructure of the city's urban and economic planning became more and more a reflection of historical currents impinging upon the city from outside and ultimately transforming even the most mundane habits, houses, and friendships of city residents.[42]

Migrations and tourism filled the boulevards with strangers; department stores dramatically displaying and selling wares from foreign shores filled the salon with exotica; photographic albums filled the eyes and the imagination with spectacles from the far corners of the earth. But these faraway places, everywhere implied, were really available to Parisians only by their *traces:* a picture here, an object there. The city itself, like a Universal Exposition, became a repository of signs, "constantly referring elsewhere," simultaneously denoting both presence and absence.[43] A fragment of the world, with everything converging upon it and circulating through it the way traffic circulated around the Etoile, Paris in the nineteenth century was more a *passage* than a place.

In this light the city itself seems to be embodied in the dynamism of the grand boulevards, and the emerging visual and perceptual patterns evident in, for instance, Le Secq's *Flying Buttresses, Reims Cathedral* and the construction photographs of Delmaet and Durandelle become metaphoric mirrors of an era. This is made even more obvious when comparing several works by E. Baldus. Born in Westphalia, Baldus trained as a painter and (after living for a while in New York in the 1840s) was a practicing photographer in France by 1849. The photographer achieved much official recognition and was hired by the govern-

fig 2.[9]
E. Baldus, *The Louvre from the Pavillon de la Bibliothèque
to the Pavillon de Marsan*, c. 1855 (Bibliothèque Nationale, Paris)

ment on several occasions to do major commissions. Among his best known bodies of work is the project he did on commission for the Ministry of the Interior: a documentary record of work in progress on the Louvre, which included both its renovation and its union with the Tuileries. The series was published in a five-volume set after construction was completed in 1857.

By necessity, given the assignment, most of the pictures are very much straightforward architectural documents *(fig. 2.⁸)* or object-oriented works; much of the series, in fact, consists of hundreds of records of sculptural details of the Louvre's new facade. But one image from about 1855, of *The Louvre from the Pavillon de la Bibliothèque to the Pavillon de Marsan (fig. 2.⁹)*, which is a view of the building from an oblique angle that emphasizes its extraordinary length, its perspectival distortions and foreshortenings, suggests another way of seeing this structure: a way of seeing that transforms the solid mass of the building into a seemingly infinite sweep of lines into deep space whose dynamism is enhanced by the repetition of architectural forms. Here Baldus's old and venerable Louvre visually recreates the modernist aims of Haussmann's urban plan— a match of sensibilities even more evident when the image is compared with the same photographer's *Clermont Station (fig. 2.¹⁰)*. Part of an album commissioned by the Baron James de Rothschild to document the opening of the Paris-to-Boulogne railroad line (chap. 6), this picture has as its central subject the tracks: those measured, relational channels of movement that provided the inspirational models for the prefect's cannonshot boulevards.

The analogies, both physical and spiritual, between the rails and the modern urban street seem obvious when *Clermont Station* is juxtaposed with another image, this time one by Adolphe Braun: the *Rue de Rivoli (fig. 2.¹¹)*, taken in or after 1855. One of a series of street photographs produced by this artist, best known for his successful business in travel photography and art reproduction, the Rue de Rivoli is centered and seen from above, moving precipitously back into depth, its arcades and gas lamps marking space as surely as did the railroad ties. Filling the sidewalks and the streets are the promeneurs, the famous Parisian prowlers who meander through the landscape of Balzac's novels, Baude-

fig 2.[10]
E. Baldus, *Clermont Station,* from *Chemin de fer du Nord,* 1855
(Bibliothèque Nationale, Paris)

fig 2.[11]
A. Braun, *Rue de Rivoli*, 1855 or after (Metropolitan Museum of Art,
David Hunter McAlpin Fund, 1947, New York)

fig 2.[12]
A. Braun, *Licorice Water Seller, Rue Castiglione, Paris,* 1855 or after
(Metropolitan Museum of Art, David Hunter McAlpin Fund, 1947, New York)

laire's poetry, and the Impressionists' paintings, and who here, on foot or on wheels, soil their boots in the muddy macadam of the nineteenth-century urban experience.

These street photographs are unusual, even revolutionary, for their time, early experiments with newly perfected techniques that made instantaneous views possible. Embodiments of the "gastronomy of the eye," the absolute relativism of vision that Richard Sennett feels defines bourgeois culture,[44] this series of pictures marks the passage of Braun-the-voyeur as he roams the city, noting street vendors and sweepers, major monuments and mundane gestures, fine waistcoats and workers' smocks *(fig. 2.¹²)*. A flaneur armed with the means to capture those images that please his eye and mind, this artist has left us with the traces of his travels through the urban wilderness—visual markers that are often, however, uncomfortably inconclusive. Take, for instance, the image entitled *The Bridge (fig. 2.¹³)*. Probably a detail of a larger work, this segment of sight has been blown up, magnified for scrutiny. Unaware of the viewer/photographer, four men, spread horizontally across the picture plane, are seen from the rear. Leaning downward in intense concentration, these Peeping Toms (united in their rapt attention in spite of the differences in their social class, a real "family of eyes") stare fixedly over the low wall of the bridge into the water. At what? That we do not, and will never, know. Unlike Charles Nègre, whose *Fallen Horse (fig. 2.¹⁴)* shows us both the rubberneckers and the focus of their attention, Braun neglects to tell us anything about this situation, wrested as it is out of its context in time and space: this passing moment, frozen, will not reveal its mysteries to our gaze. A fragment of time like Paris is a fragment of space, this picture, like the city it depicts, is a slice of life, constantly referring elsewhere, simultaneously denoting presence and absence.

"In that black or luminous square," Baudelaire wrote, "life lives, life dreams, life suffers."[45] He was talking about closed windows, those frames onto people's private lives that provided him with a chance not only to look but to create—to leave the confines of his own existence through the medium of thought in order to invent and thus vicariously experience another's story. But

fig 2.[13]

A. Braun, *The Bridge, Paris* 1855 or after (Metropolitan Museum of Art, David Hunter McAlpin Fund, 1947, New York)

fig 2.[14]

C. Nègre, *Fallen Horse, Quai Bourbon, Paris,* c. 1851
(Museum of Modern Art, New York)

the "luminous square" to which he refers could just as well be the frame of a photograph like *The Bridge,* an implied but unfulfilled narrative that must be completed in the viewer's mind. Baudelaire's famous fantasy life, his insistent projection of his own thought onto others, was not only an opium-induced trait; it was, rather, characteristic of the same age that gave us documentary photography. Frozen snippets of life that, severed from their roots in time and space, refuse to reveal their secrets, these sun pictures embody the puzzle of public life in Paris in the nineteenth century. Filling our eyes with visual stimulation, with the "attitudes and gestures of living beings," [46] these images are invitations to dream, to explain, to fulfill a narrative ambience that becomes more mystifying the more it is fleshed out with documentary detail. Small wonder that Walter Benjamin equated *flânerie* with imagination: the chronotope of Second Empire Paris was a dreamscape whose details loomed as large as mushrooms in Alice's Wonderland.

As they do in Adolphe Braun's extraordinary series of pictures of traffic streaming across the Pont Neuf *(figs. 2.[15], 2.[16], 2.[17]).* Or rather: Braun's single image of this bridge — momentarily frozen and preserved — that is selectively blown up, scrutinized, and magnified in small bits that bloom like Alice's mushrooms. There were artists, like Henri Le Secq for instance, in his documentation of various cathedrals, who understood and utilized the cinematic possibilities of photography during this period, and who therefore left us with sequences of images that follow the footsteps (and therefore the viewpoint) of a promeneur as he or she would have approached, moved around, and scrutinized a subject. But this narrative sequencing, which moves forward in time and space, is different from Braun's isolation and magnification of detail, as if he were parsing a second in order to reveal the eternal structure of the transitory. The original frozen moment in *Pont Neuf* is fixed, it can't move in either time or space and there is no sequel to extend it in one or the other dimension. But this existential event can be dissected, stared at, toyed with, or enlarged, as one wishes, once it has been trapped in the freeze-frame of a photo, and this scopophiliac control was obviously Braun's aim.

fig 2.[15]

A. Braun, *Pont Neuf, Paris,* 1855 or after (Metropolitan Museum of Art, David Hunter McAlpin Fund, 1947, New York)

Like Balzac, this photographer was fixating on a body, a gesture, a cut of clothing: those odd details, like the man lounging on the seat at the side of the bridge, that one does not necessarily notice on first viewing. Balzac inflated minutiae in such a way that it seemed connected to everything else in the social world. Like the impressionist critic Edmond Duranty, he asked a fragment to embody within itself the larger social forces of nineteenth-century Parisian life. "By means of a back," Duranty wrote, "we want a temperament, an age, a social condition to be revealed."[47] Braun's photographs isolate that back; his images give us the illusion of a closer look, a clearer eye. But ultimately, of course, this is an illusion, because these fragmentary glimpses of conventionalized gestures and clothes reveal only so much before their isolated details begin to destroy rather than enrich the larger picture, to deplete rather than enhance the global meanings. Like Manet and Degas, those masters of transitory gestures whose intentions are unclear, Braun shows us the ambiguity of our bodies in time and space, those social masks that simultaneously pierce and reinforce the sheer impenetrability of the real. No matter how hard we stare or how close we get, these enlargements remain a puzzle, "a fragment whose existence never exceeds the fragment."[48] These passersby are not synthesized into the larger metaphoric vision of a Balzac. Instead, their absolute particularity fills the frame, inviting and simultaneously remaining impervious to explication and completion.

This imperviousness, of course, brings us back to the moral universe of "The Eyes of the Poor," that landscape where people keep flickering in and out of focus. Faced with what he thought was intimacy, Baudelaire hit a wall—the same barrier confronted by Adolphe Braun as he attempted to move in close, to penetrate the web of illusion that defines the real. This wall was an issue in Second Empire Paris, where a stable truth was hard to find: the city that disappeared and reappeared as something different, where neighborhoods that once were home became, in the blink of an eye, the impersonal meeting and marketplaces for the world. Filled with foreigners and goods from afar that imprinted their own images on city spaces, Paris itself had become impenetrable, unrecognizable, unknowable—a surreal cityscape made strange by change, even (maybe especially) to those born there. Disoriented natives, their intimacy with their birthplace thwarted by the currents of history, were as displaced as the immigrants who arrived in Paris and stayed, assuming a resident outsider status that destroyed all fixed social concepts of space: of what Rob Shields calls "the (distant) foreign and the (local) intimate."[49]

In a public arena so fraught with confusion, one couldn't tell the players (even those one knew best) without a score card, and much of the artistic production of this period was an attempt to both describe and cognitively map a landscape whose parameters had become so fluid yet so charged with the ex-

fig 2.[16]
A. Braun, *Pont Neuf, Paris,* detail, 1855 or after (Metropolitan Museum of Art,
David Hunter McAlpin Fund, 1947, New York)

fig 2.[17]

A. Braun, *Pont Neuf, Paris*, detail, 1855 or after (Metropolitan Museum of Art,
David Hunter McAlpin Fund, 1947, New York)

panded socioeconomic relations of modernism. The urban environment became a series of disconnected, often fragmentary, image bites; the spectacles of the city, like the goods in the Universal Expositions and the new department stores, were there to be consumed. The flaneur, faced with this overwhelming visual display, had two choices, represented by the two "observation modes" assumed by the narrator in Edgar Allan Poe's "The Man of the Crowd," a story translated by Baudelaire, which was influential on the French artists of this period. At first Poe's convalescent narrator rests apart from the crowd, content to be a passive spectator, connecting to the press of humanity only by the act of the vision and the medium of thought. But soon he realizes he can plunge into the vortex, mix with the swarm, let his body follow his eyesight as if vision itself were the *primum mobile* of action. Seduced by the sight of a bizarre, inscrutable man, Poe's narrator finally chooses the latter course—to no avail, since his active pursuit of the truth ultimately leads him down a blind alley. Having at last penetrated the body public, this man emerges from the maelstrom with no more information than before; he too hits a wall, which calls into question all his former certainty about the possibilities of human understanding—and human decency. The wall he encounters marks the boundaries of the socially acceptable. Beyond this barrier are only "books that do not permit themselves to be read, . . . secrets that do not permit themselves to be told." [50] This was a wilderness peopled only by those criminals and savages who play such a large role in the nineteenth-century literary imagination.

Small wonder that this *époque*—and Poe—gave us the detective novel, the literary genre that perhaps most closely parallels photography because in it, too, past actions are reconstituted by visual clues. Like Adolph Braun in his blowups of the Pont Neuf, the detective revealed the mysterious stranger lurking in the shadows as he searched for the traces of truth hidden in the corners of the social terrain. The parallel between photography and detective stories, noticed by Walter Benjamin among others, points up once again the complexity of the medium's role in nineteenth-century thought. [51] This visual tool whose claim to fame was its absolute fidelity to the physical world, its ability to transcribe and thus bear witness to this level of reality, became in fact one of the vehicles by which reality itself transmuted into the fantastic. Like Poe's narrator, the photographers entered into the crowd, they described the stranger in detail, they mapped his trajectory and traced his steps. They froze him, magnified him, zoomed in for a closer look at his fingernails or his shoes. The world became a sequence of clues: once again, what was present was a fragment, pointing to what was absent; what was visible was a trace, a trail, leading to what was not. In other words, in its revelatory capacity, photography was one of the nineteenth century's main purveyors of mystery.

Besides the detective, there was another literary figure of this period who perceived the physical world as a sequence of revelatory clues: the Noble Savage, that archetypal Other brought to Parisians by the American novels of James Fenimore Cooper. The kinship between natives of the New World and the man of the crowd—both of them men on the edge, "walking through society's laws"—was remarked upon in an article of 1846 attributed to Balzac or Hippolyte Castine.[52] Slightly later, Baudelaire would nostalgically characterize the savage, the New World counterpart to the dandy, as "the *dernier éclat* of heroism among decadence;"[53] and Alexandre Dumas would write *The Mohicans of Paris,* a potboiler about urban natives seen as the French counterpart to Cooper's *The Last of the Mohicans.*[54] The Noble Savage, like the old Paris, was threatened with imminent extinction; a native about to be displaced as surely as the native of Paris had been by Haussmann, he too suffered from the temporal and spatial disjunctions that were spleen. The Mohican represented the hero about to be vanquished by outside forces' unstoppable incursions into the world of which he had formerly been master. To the artists of the Second Empire, therefore, he was a brother, an alter ego—and they had little trouble transposing his territory onto their own.

"The Savages of Cooper right in Paris!" wrote Paul Féval in 1863. "Are not the great squares as mysterious as forests of the New World?"[55] Balzac, in *Splendeurs et Misères des Courtisanes,* took that analogy even further. "You see," he wrote, "Paris is like a forest in the New World, where a score of savages roam—the Illinois, the Hurons, who live on the proceeds offered them by the different social classes. You are a hunter of millions; to capture your millions you use snares, limed twigs, decoys. Some hunt heiresses, others a legacy; some fish for conscience, others sell their clients bound hand and foot. The man who comes back with his gamebag well stocked is hailed, feted, received in good society." [56] The savage, until the end, survived by skill, cunning—and hyperactive visual acumen. Like the detective, the flaneur, and the photographer, he trafficked in detail, and his very life depended on his ability to read the clues and signs of his environment.

Cooper's native American heroes and villains make their way through the virgin forest by deciphering those markers known only to the initiated. Like the detective, the savage can reconstruct past events and predict future ones based on the appearance of a footprint, a broken branch, or a feather. Their environment "speaks" through visual clues and natives "listen" with their eyes as well as their ears; in this world where even a slight shift in body language can determine the outcome of a battle, every sign becomes bloated with meanings and correspondences. The superhuman attention to detail necessary for survival in Cooper's universe, "where every broken branch is either disturbing or cause for hope, where every tree trunk hides an enemy gun or the bow of an invisible and silent avenger," [57] obviously made a major impression on Balzac, who in turn scanned the urban horizon with his novelist's gaze, scouting out parallel symbols of warfare and cunning in the mire of the macadam: "The poetry of terror that the stratagems of warring enemy tribes spread throughout the American forests . . . can be associated with the smallest details of Parisian life. The passersby, the boutiques, the hackney cabs, a woman standing at a crossing: everything offered . . . the enormous interest that a tree trunk, a beaver lodge, a rock, a bison skin, a motionless canoe or foliage reflected in water evokes in a novel by Cooper." [58] Paris, metaphorically speaking, *became* a wilderness; the virgin forest, that outpost of empire under siege in Cooper's books, moved (like the immigrants and their foreign goods) into the very heart of the metropolis. The empire, transformed, became the emporium, ready to be possessed: visually, economically,

fig 2.[18]

H. Bayard, *Grocery Store,* n.d. (1840s?) (Société Française de Photographie, Paris)

fig 2.[19]

C. Nègre, *The Organ Grinder*, 1853 (Bibliothèque Nationale, Paris)

fig 2.²⁰

C. Nègre, *The Fisherwoman,* c. 1852 (Bibliothèque Nationale, Paris)

fig 2.²¹

A. A. E. Disdéri, *The Vagabond,* from *Types Photographiques,* 1853
(Bibliothèque Nationale, Paris)

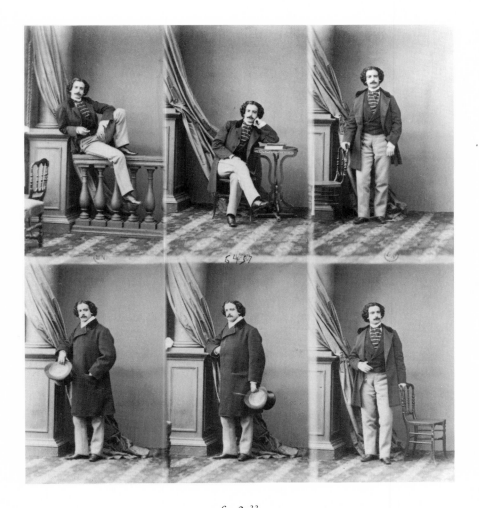

fig 2.[22]

A. A. E. Disdéri, *Young Man, 6 Times,* Carte-de-Visite, n.d. (probably 1860s)
(Bibliothèque Nationale, Paris)

and intellectually. The Hurons, the French, the Mohicans, the English, the savage, and the dandy: all of them met on the streets of the chronotope of nineteenth-century Paris, where the traces of truth were mercilessly stalked under the gas lamps, in cafés and *passages* and exhibition halls, by flaneurs and photographers alike.

But whereas the savage and the detective, those heroes of literature, sought and found a definitive truth, the clues were more ambiguous on the streets walked by Balzac and his compatriots. They roamed and transcribed, they stared and described, and the plethora of images—visual and verbal—they left behind attest to their need to exhaustively catalog the passing parade, to find the hidden signs that might explain a world rendered increasingly strange. But the family of eyes staring back at them—the grocers, the street people, the organ grinders, the gentlemen *(figs. 2.[18], 2.[19], 2.[20], 2.[21], 2.[22])*, that *Galerie Contemporaine* of faces chosen and preserved by the first generations of photographers— are but a series of projections, reflections in the eyes of the beholder. Trapped within conventionalized roles by the perambulating gaze of the artist, whether in the studio or on the sidewalk, these allusive Others will never break the boundaries of the image that is their allotted social space. Unlike the narrator's lover in "The Eyes of the Poor," they will not speak; their voice will never destroy the harmony, the smooth surface of appearances. They will be, instead, like the poor family members in the prose poem, who remain a silent chorus staring from the sidelines. Their anonymous faces will circulate endlessly through the Hall of Mirrors which defines public perception, and which insures that any genuine encounter with the stranger on the street will always be postponed.

III

Still Points in a Turning World

I

E nter the *Rue Daubenton (fig. 3.¹)*. One freeze-frame in the ongoing film of Paris street life, this view (taken from the Rue Gracieuse looking toward the Rue de la Clef) was produced around 1865 by Charles Marville. Marville at the time was in the employ of Baron Haussmann, who felt strongly that the old streets and buildings, as well as their destruction and reconstruction, should be documented as part of the city's historic records and as a way to make sure that all could recognize the extent of his own accomplishments. For this purpose he hired several archivists whose association took the official name of City Council Permanent Subcommittee on Historic Works. These archivists, in turn, advised Marville, who became the "photographe de la ville de Paris." [1]

Rue Daubenton is a classic old street — one of the many recorded by this diligent worker who was assigned to photograph according to Haussmann's plan and to include before, during, and after shots of the areas in question. The street was only so named in 1864, after the eighteenth-century naturalist Louis Daubenton. Before that, it had been called Rue d'Orleans-Saint-Marcel. This particular neighborhood in the Fifth Arrondissement was much disrupted by the piercing of the Rue Monge nearby. In fact, the very intersection where Marville stood to take this photograph was doomed to disappear around 1870, when the part of the Rue Gracieuse that linked up with Rue Daubenton was demolished.[2] So this picture falls into the "before" category, the body of work by this photographer that is best known and best loved by those who yearn nostalgically for times gone by. It represents a particular moment in the history of this street, yet a moment that implies many others. Marville preserved what was, and what still is, in 1865; but just his presence there, his singling out of this site for documentation and thus photographic preservation, signals its ruin. For he was Haussmann's advance man, and the hand that pointed the camera also pointed the finger of death.

Clearly, this picture stands in a complex relationship to time: to the past, present, and future of the city, to an urge for preservation that accompanied a stronger urge for destruction and renewal. In saving this ancient street for us, Marville turned a physical reality into a memory that has outlived its physical counterpart. The long exposure time necessary to make this photograph stopped time, metaphorically speaking; we can still see the old cobblestones, the old shops, the old gutters, and even a few of the old people, long since dead, who stood still long enough to register on his wet collodion plates with exposures of 3 to 12 seconds. Marville's decision to work with such long exposure times was a choice; there were faster processes available at the time, processes that allowed people like Adolphe Braun (see chap. 2) and the popular stereographic photographers to capture the activity of the crowds and traffic on the street. But the instantaneous view was not for Marville, the official photographer of the city of Paris. This man was making history, and history had to last.

Part of Marville's assignment was to photograph in such a way that Haussmann's future accomplishments could be appreciated. Thus he inevitably chose vantage points emphasizing the twisting, the narrowness, the ill repair,

fig 3.[1]
C. Marville, *Rue Daubenton*, c. 1865
(Bibliothèque Historique de la Ville de Paris, Paris)

and the claustrophobia of the medieval streets. *Rue Daubenton* was taken from the side of the road, a point of view that allowed his audience to best see the meanderings and impasses of the block. The street curves off to the right in the distance, but Marville's vantage point makes it seem as if the building in the background was an obstruction, the type of obstruction that would never encumber Haussmann's broad straight streets with their long vistas. The point of view is low enough to reinforce this sense of closure; the cobblestones—like the signs, the fences, the street lamps, the fabrics, the hay, and the peelings of paint on the walls—pop out at us as detail that emphasizes the clutter. The few people visible, in the doorways or behind the grills of the windows, seem to be trapped on the sidelines, shunted off to the right and left of the picture. Only the street, however crooked, is clear space.

But the street was, of course, not really clear. In this picture as in many of Marville's photographs of Paris, there are barely visible traces of "ghosts:" those people who were moving too fast to register on Marville's plates. This photographer's images record a time zone different from the one inhabited by these passersby. The traffic, the hustle and bustle, the street life for which Paris has always been famous: these were not his interests. Marville was defining the city in different terms—the same terms used by his "boss."

The streets that were so central to the baron's urban planning were to become central to the photographs of "Haussmann's man," as Maria Morris Hambourg has called Charles Marville.[3] And they are literally central, as one can see by looking at *Rue Daubenton,* which depicts a street going off into deep space in the middle of the picture plane, with the buildings, cafés, shops, and signs lining it on the sides. This in itself was a novel pictorial structure, one very different from many of the more object-oriented photographs that Marville took for Louis Blanquart-Evrard's albums published in the 1850s *(fig. 3.²).* Unlike Hippolyte Bayard, the clerk who played a large role in the invention of photography and who spent decades focusing on city streets with and without crowds of people on them *(fig. 3.³),* Marville began his career conservatively, by creating and selling typical views of Paris. These earlier pictures generally have monu-

fig 3.²

C. Marville, *Apse of Notre-Dame de Paris,* 1853 (Bibliothèque Nationale, Paris)

ments, buildings, fountains, or sculptures as their central subjects; the streets, where they are visible, serve only as backdrops, or signs of the larger urban context within which these monuments exist. In the photographs done for the city in the 1860s, however, Marville changed his focus to fit his new assignment *(figs. 3.⁴, 3.⁵, 3.⁶).* His subjects are now the streets themselves: the means of transport, the channel of relationship between objects, the dynamic arteries in a circulatory network that was coming into being.

But there is a profound contradiction at the heart of these photographs of the streets of Paris. In spite of their emphasis on the channels of circulation, the pictures themselves obstinately refuse to move. *Rue Daubenton,* like all the

fig 3.[3]

H. Bayard, *Rue de la Gendarmerie,* n.d.
(Bibliothèque Historique de la Ville de Paris, Paris)

fig 3.⁴

C. Marville, *Rue Estienne,* n.d.
(Bibliothèque Historique de la Ville de Paris, Paris)

fig 3.[5]

C. Marville, *Rue des Innocents,* n.d. (Musée Carnavalet, Paris)

fig 3.[6]

C. Marville, *Rue Gracieuse*, n.d. (Musée Carnavalet, Paris)

others, is absolutely static. This is in part because of Marville's insistence on classically balanced pictorial form: the street is centered, the buildings line it on each side, and the structure in the background keeps the eye from wandering aimlessly into deep space. The eye wanders just so far and no farther, and everything it lights upon—from the signs, to the architecture, to the cafés and the merchandise on display—is still. There are four people depicted here: two in the door of the café at the right, one on the sidewalk farther to the rear, and one leaning out of a second-story window on the left. Yet because of the long exposure time, they, like the streetlights and fences, don't move; they too become

fig 3.[7]

C. Marville, *The Piercing of the Avenue de l'Opéra,* c. 1865 (Bibliothèque Historique de la Ville de Paris, Paris)

fig 3.[8]

C. Marville, *Place du Châtelet*, 1858 (Musée Carnavalet, Paris)

inanimate objects, fixtures of the neighborhood. Even Marville's demolition photographs, like *The Piercing of the Avenue de L'Opera (fig. 3.⁷)* and *Place du Châtelet, (fig. 3.⁸)*, are notable for their lack of activity. One sees workers, piles of rubble, half-demolished buildings and construction sites—all the signposts of hustle and bustle, destruction and creation. But the pictures themselves are static, silent, still—more markedly and obstinately so than would have been necessary to comply with the standards for architectural or construction photography (like pictures by A. Collard, *fig. 3.⁹*, P. Petit, *fig. 3.¹⁰*, and the studio of Delmaet and Durandelle discussed in chap. 2) of the time. Each one is a *nature morte*, a "dead nature," to translate literally from the French. Marville's Paris was dead before Haussmann got to it, as if a neutron bomb had wiped out all signs of animate life and left only inanimate buildings, spaces, and urban furnishings—the traces of culture.

It is in these traces of culture that Marville's definition of the city, his Paris, lies. For the urban experience he depicts has nothing to do with people per se, but only with the things they create, wear out, destroy, and then rebuild. His pictures chronicle the evolution of physical change in objects and spaces, which is why it is important to keep in mind that this photographer was not thinking in terms of individual photographs. Every one of his pictures of Paris is a documentary record of one stage in a *process*. Each picture represents a moment that is either before, during, or after Haussmann and his henchmen arrived. According to Marie de Thézy, an image like *Rue Daubenton* would generally have been one of two photographs—taken from two different vantage points—of each street scheduled for demolition, and it would have been followed by a series of pictures of the site in successive stages of its reconstruction.[4] These working methods make it clear that one loses sight of the larger meaning of Marville's street works if one does not look at them as an ensemble, as a series chronicling, first and foremost, the process of change in space over time.

Seeing Marville's Paris photographs as serial images allows one to perceive single prints, like *Rue Daubenton,* as variations on a theme that has a much larger conceptual context. It also helps to explain the obsessive repeti-

fig 3.[9]
A. Collard, *Pont Louis-Philippe*, n.d. (Bibliothèque Nationale, Paris)

tiousness of this body of work—and here I am referring very specifically to the street photographs, independent of the series on specific buildings and urban furnishings he also produced as part of this project *(figs. 3.[11], 3.[12])*. Marville took thousands of pictures of the streets of Paris, and after a while, except for the details of various streets and shops, they all blur together, they all seem the same. The subjects of the pictures—the streets, the architecture, the urban furnishings, and travaux when applicable—remain the same, and the photographer's chosen point of view on them varies only within a very small range. The photographs are almost identical in pictorial structure: a street lined with buildings (or shacks and vacant lots in the less densely populated outlying areas of the city, *fig. 3.[13]*) is at the center of the picture plane and moves back into space; sometimes the street curves to the right, sometimes to the left, sometimes it goes straight back. Often the photographer stands in the middle of the block, though occasionally a *place* or a crossroad can be seen in the foreground. But these are

fig 3.[10]

P. Petit, from the *Photographic Album of the Building of the Universal Exposition of 1867*, June 27, 1866 (Bibliothèque Historique de la Ville de Paris, Paris)

fig 3.[11]

C. Marville, *Streetlight, Pont du Carrousel,* n.d.
(Bibliothèque Historique de la Ville de Paris, Paris)

fig 3.[12]

C. Marville, *Office of the Omnibus Company, Place de la Bourse,* c. 1866
(Bibliothèque Historique de la Ville de Paris, Paris)

fig 3.[13]

C. Marville, *Rue Champlain*, c. 1865 (Musée Carnavalet, Paris)

fig 3.[14]

C. Marville, *Avenue des Gobelins,* n.d.
(Bibliothèque Historique de la Ville de Paris, Paris)

minor variations on the same formal construct, and ultimately they do nothing to alleviate the overwhelming impression of sameness one has when one looks at the street pictures. This is clearly not because Marville was by definition a boring or one-idea photographer; nor can it necessarily be attributed to Hauss-mann's assignment, since Marville's pictures of the park, the Bois de Boulogne, possibly done as part of the same documentary project, are diversified in subject, vantage point, and mood, and they lack the clinical feeling that pervades his images of the city streets.

Rather, it seems that the repetitiousness of the photographs represents a choice on the part of the photographer—a choice intimately bound up with the images' static emptiness. If these pictures do not move, if their subjects do not move or change—neither, it seems, does the photographer. Looking at hundreds of Marvilles all together, one gets the impression that his camera stays stationary, and the world changes around it. For the objects and spaces do change—drastically—from picture to picture: crooked alleyways are replaced by broad, straight streets; small crumbling buildings are transformed into larger, modern structures; and the human scale of homey details seen in *Rue Dauben-ton* gives way to the regularity of identical apartments, tree-lined boulevards, and arcades that subsume the particular into a more generalized urban rhythm *(figs. 3.¹⁴, 3.¹⁵)*. Each one of these frozen moments is a piece of a larger pattern taking place over time, and the repetitiousness of the pictures allows the viewer to gauge exactly what has transpired in the days, weeks, months, and even years *between* them. Marville, the photographer, bore static witness to this process, and this passivity marks him as truly "Haussmann's man." For his photographs represent the new concept of urbanism taking shape in Paris in the 1860s, a new definition of a city in which objects and spaces embody within themselves changes that seem to have little to do with personal, people-oriented activity or will.

This new urbanism was, of course, "Haussmannization." By the mid 1860s, Haussmann's *grands travaux* were far enough along to have made a substantial change in the face, and the life, of the city. It was during this period that

fig 3.[15]
C. Marville, *Rue de Rivoli,* c. 1870–1871
(Bibliothèque Historique de la Ville de Paris, Paris)

fig 3.[16]

A. Houssin, *Place du Château d'Eau,* 1863 (Bibliothèque Nationale, Paris)

photographers, city residents, and tourists alike were forced to grapple with the implications of the urban spaces that, for better or worse, were now their own. And this brings us to another photograph, a stereographic instantaneous view of the *Place du Château d'eau (fig. 3.*[16]*)*, taken by a man named Auguste-Lange Houssin on December 24, 1863—in other words, at roughly the same time that Marville produced *Rue Daubenton*.

I I

We know little about Monsieur Houssin, or any of the other commercial stereographic street photographers who worked in Paris during this time, for that matter. We are left only with their photographs, such as those in the massive collection at the Bibliothèque Nationale in Paris, and the survival of so many images attests to their great popularity as cultural artifacts during these years. These men were working in a very different milieu from that of people like Gustave Le Gray, Henri Le Secq, and Charles Nègre, those well-known personalities in the photographic art community in the 1850s. In fact, the original "artistic photography" movement seems to have dissipated, or at least lost much of its impetus and many of its members, by the 1860s, and into this void stepped the popular image makers like Adolphe Disdéri and the stereo photographers, enterprising opportunists who made their fortunes by widely distributing their images to the general public rather than to a more sophisticated or elitist audience.

Interestingly enough, in their divorce from elitist art practices, men like Houssin share common ground with Marville. According to Marie de Thézy, Marville never became a member of the French Photographers' Society and was not a regular participant in their exhibitions.[5] Marville, too, was primarily a commercial photographer, but whereas he worked for the government during the 1860s, the stereographic photographers were attempting to corner their share of the speculative popular market. Both were, by necessity, very aware of the social and economic impulses of their time. And by choosing, as their central tasks, the visual interpretation of Paris, both committed themselves to participating in the redefinition of urban space that Haussmann had begun.

It is useful, in this context, to see M. Houssin and his colleagues as the visual counterparts of the people who wrote the Paris guidebooks of the 1860s. The city was, at the time, a popular tourist destination. As was discussed in chapter 2, the rebuilding of the urban landscape, the Universal Expositions of 1855 and 1867, the prosperity reflected in the shops, the cafés, and the early department stores: all contributed to making the city an attractive place to visit. The guidebooks, with their maps and practical information as well as their overview of social and cultural life, painted a visual and verbal picture of the new Paris to lead the tourist through the unfamiliar terrain. The role of the stereo photographs, on the other hand, was both more direct and more complex. Cheap and easily obtained on the streets of the city, they provided visitors with mementos of their trip. But, like picture postcards, they also served as guides to what was important. By singling out certain monuments and scenes, they helped to shape the popular vision of this new capital of France. Clearly, no commercial image maker could stay in business by photographing sites that were not of interest to the general public; but it is also true that the existence of numerous photographic images worked to mark a site, a monument, a particular type of scene as exemplary of a given place. The stereographic photographers, therefore, formulated the visual clichés of the new Paris of the 1860s. In this context, the existence of so many pictures, like Houssin's *Place du Château d'eau,* of the streets and street life of Paris, is an indication that such scenes were considered, by the general public of the time, as characteristic of the City of Light.

The photograph itself is a characteristic example of this genre of images. Taken from a high vantage point so the viewer gains an overview of the scene, it depicts the open space of the *place* and the traffic upon it, as well as a large building at the rear (barracks for 2,000 military men, built for security reasons by Haussmann at the exact site where Daguerre's Diorama had been;

this neighborhood, a workers' enclave close to the Bastille, was a revolutionary center throughout the nineteenth century). The exact opposite of Marville's classically balanced scene, everything in this picture works to emphasize movement. The point of view sets the building at an angle, which converges with the diagonal, left-to-right sweep of the street as it pushes back into deep space. The eye follows the direction of the pedestrians and carriages in its initial scanning of the image. A secondary vortex of movement, however, is provided on the left by the fountain, the Château d'eau designed by Girard and inaugurated in 1811 under Napoleon I. The concentric circles of the fountain seem to spin energy around them, discharging it toward the semicircular line of trees that converges with the traffic, once again, at the right rear.

This emphasis on action is appropriate, for this *place* (now the Place de la République) was designed for just that purpose. Created in 1862 after Haussmann's "piercing" of the Boulevard Voltaire and the Rue de la République, the *place* marks the point where these two new roads meet the old Boulevard du Temple. The wide open spaces and broad streets were designed to permit large amounts of traffic and easy circulation, and if one looks to the top right of the picture one can see, very clearly, the lines that divide the old medieval city from Haussmann's new plan. Even on the level of scale, the differences are obvious. The new *place* provides monumental buildings, broad boulevards, and wide open spaces, contrasting sharply with the small structures and narrow, cluttered streets of yesteryear. Merely looking at the anonymous traffic on these thoroughfares, one understands how, and why, Haussmann conceived his circulatory scheme.

In many ways, therefore, Houssin's stereograph is the antithesis of Marville's *Rue Daubenton*. First and foremost, Marville depicts an old Parisian street, whereas Houssin has chosen to celebrate the new. Marville took a street-level vantage point that emphasizes the closure of the scene, whereas Houssin's above-ground view (not to mention the 3-D stereo effect) opens up the space and allows the eye to sweep over the entire area. Marville's composition is centered, static, and balanced, whereas Houssin's is full of active diagonals, vortexes of energy, and subjects (both buildings and people) that have been "cut" by the frame, thus signaling that this is a "slice of life" that implies a much larger scene. To carry this contrast further, Marville chose to use a long exposure time, while Houssin capitalized on the technical advances of the 1850s and 1860s that made instantaneous views possible—and that allowed him to capture the hustle and bustle of the traffic on the new streets.

The activity of street traffic is important here, not only because of its obvious connections to Haussmannization but also because of what it implies about movement—and thus time and space—in Paris in the nineteenth century. This period saw an influx not only of tourists but also of new residents to the city. This was in part because of the economic incentive of jobs on the public works projects, but it was also directly related to the development of the rail-roads. The first train left Paris in 1837, and by 1855 France had completed the rail link between the capital and the Mediterranean. One of the major reasons given for Haussmann's restructuring of Paris was to make the city easily acces-sible by train and easily negotiable after one arrived at the new railway terminals. The city streets, therefore, owed at least part of their final form to the railroad networks, and any discussion of people on the boulevards must deal with the new modes of transportation that brought them there.

In fact, Haussmann's urban plan, with its emphasis on circulation, was a symptom, not a cause, of much more widespread cultural and technological change. As is obvious in certain documentary photographs from this period by E. Fixon and others (fig. 3.¹⁷), railroad tracks were laid to aid the construction of the new streets—whose regular rhythms and endless expanses were, there-fore, echoes of the rails initially used to trace their trajectory. But the national railroad system, with its speed much greater than that attainable by either hu-man or horse power, telescoped space and time even more drastically than the new network of Parisian boulevards: a trip that might have taken days on horse-back took only hours on the train. This artificial extension of human range was reiterated by the invention of the telegraph, an important tool of the railway network; coming into use at the Paris Bourse in 1852, it allowed messages to be

fig 3.[17]
E. Fixon, *Piercing of the Avenue Daumesnil*, 1862
(Société Française de la Photographie, Paris)

transmitted with great rapidity but without the intervention of a human courier. Such new technological inventions altered the very concept of movement, which became in these contexts mechanical rather than experiential: machines did what humans had formerly done, only faster and thus better. And possibly more important, while movement had once implied human or animal locomotion, it now took on a new *passivity*. Where before people walked or rode toward things, now bodies hurtled through space like parcels, and things themselves began to come toward people with an alarming speed and a seeming lack of individual control.

There are few more graphic descriptions of reactions to these changes than the passage in Zola's *La Bête Humaine* where Jacques the trainman talks to his Aunt Phasie, who is sick and isolated in the countryside:

The train that had been signaled, the slow, leaving Paris at 12:45 P.M., could be heard coming a long way off with a dull roar. Then it emerged from the tunnel with a sudden loud beat echoing through the countryside, and passed with its thunderous wheels and the mass of its coaches, invincible, powerful as a hurricane.

"Mum, you grumble about never seeing even a cat in this hole. But look at all those people."

At first she failed to understand, and said in surprise:

"People, where? Oh, yes, those people going by. A fat lot of good! I don't know them from Adam, and can't talk to them! . . . No, no, that's no way to see people."

Yet this idea of the tide of people that the up and down trains bore along past her every day in the deep silence of her solitude left her pensive, looking at the line as night was falling. . . . It seemed funny being buried in this wilderness, without a soul to confide in, when day and night, all the time, so many men and women were rushing past in the thunder of trains shaking the house, and then tearing away at full speed. It was a fact that all the world went by, not only French people but foreigners too, people from the most distant lands, since nowadays nobody could stay at home and all the nations, it was said, would soon be only one. That was progress, all brothers together, all going along to some Better Land! She tried to count them roughly, at so many per carriage, but there were too many and she couldn't keep up. Often she thought she recognized faces. . . . But they all went by in a flash and she was never quite sure she really had seen them; all the faces got blurred and merged into one another, indistinguishable. The torrent rushed on, leaving nothing behind. What depressed her so much was the feeling that, behind all this nonstop movement and all the comfort and money going by, the breathless crowd had no idea she was there, in danger of death. So if her man finished her off one night, the trains would go on passing each other near her dead body without even suspecting the crime in this lonely house.[6]

Phasie lays there dying—while all the world rushes by. Movement is something that happens *around* her, *to* her. It is the "thunder," the "flash," the "torrent" that is "powerful as a hurricane" or an act of God or nature—that is, in fact, in direct opposition to her own passivity. Marville's stationary camera, which bears mute witness to a world that seems to undergo change without human assistance, takes on new meaning in the light of this passage, but so do the faceless crowds that people Houssin's *Place du Château d'eau*. For Phasie's comments point up with emphatic clarity the new social interactions engendered by the new means of transportation: where once proximity in space meant human interaction, the new patterns of mobility now rendered that impossible.

This was as true on the city streets as on the railroad lines. In 1828, the omnibuses, the first public transportation system in Paris, began operating (see *fig. 3.*[12]*)*. In these transports, as in crowded restaurants and cafés, department stores and *passages* filled with strangers, people stared at each other without speaking, enjoying the spectacle without active involvement. These new, purely visual relationships, which had nothing to do with acquaintance or even polite conversation, came to fruition on Haussmann's boulevards, the stomping ground of the anonymous crowd. The broad promenades made the streets a natural place of congregation—for everyone. People of different classes, nationalities, backgrounds, and professions rubbed shoulders in public. But their synchronicity in time and space was a cover for a new, truly modern form of alienation, which permitted anonymous visual contact as the only form of human exchange.

The flaneur took on the role of the silent observer whose inner life could be enriched by the city only to the extent that he remained physically and verbally aloof from it. Passivity, in other words, became the key to the urban experience. As Richard Sennett has explained, "The public man as passive spectator was a man released and freed. He was released from the burdens of respectability he carried in the home, and even more, he was released from action itself. Passive silence in public is a means of withdrawal; to the extent that silence can be enforced, to that extent every person is free of the social bond itself." [7] Paradoxically, as geographical distance was bridged by technological advancement, the gaps between people, their social distance, yawned wider than ever before. A photographer like Houssin is, in a sense, the apotheosis of this social voyeurism; his camera records, but doesn't otherwise relate to or interact with, these nameless passersby—the tiny, antlike promeneurs, the people who make up the "breathless crowds" in *Place du Château d'eau,* and who are fundamentally no less isolated, from the photographer or each other, than Phasie herself.

One can see this by looking closely at Houssin's photographs—and not only because of his promeneurs' small size, social distance, and lack of contact. One can see it by examining the structure of the stereographic photographers' overall bodies of work. This picture, like Marville's *Rue Daubenton,* is part of an ensemble, and the stereographic depictions of Paris streets, when seen together, are startling in their repetitious sameness. Marville repeated his pictorial structures, a stance that allowed him to manifest changes in space over time; photographers like Houssin, on the other hand, produced stock images of different streets, different places, and different people from the same point of view, and in the process homogenized them all. Here we can examine the specifics of the Place du Château d'eau, but when this *place* is seen in the midst of hundreds of similar streets—all of them straight and wide, all of them the primary subject of the image as they move back into deep space (most often on the diagonal), all of them seen from an elevated point of view, and all of them busy with traffic *(figs. 3.[18], 3.[19], 3.[20], 3.[21])*—one's perception of the individuality of this particular locale changes drastically. For these popular images are more about patterns than they are about specific urban spaces. Each one of the streets they depict is simply a piece of a larger metropolitan system, which has uniformity and regularity as its theme. The network of boulevards depicted by Houssin and his competitors is as faceless as the anonymous crowd that peoples it; all of these roads serve one purpose—to effectively channel movement—and that movement is as incessant, as anonymous, as uniform, and as regular as the streets themselves. Individual people, even individualized crowds, don't exist here, anymore than do truly individualized boulevards, squares, or neighborhoods.

In a situation like this, an element of randomness comes to the fore: in *Place du Château d'eau*, certain anonymous people, it matters not who, just happened to be in the right space at the right time to be preserved for posterity. There is something fitting about this, since it was in the nineteenth century in Paris that the idea of the accidental occupation of space, at least in terms of one's home, took hold. Before this time, a (financially comfortable) family's home was its own, part of its heritage. Once buildings ceased to be the family patrimony and became instead values of exchange, part of an impersonal and speculative real estate market, and once they were considered as larger structures that could be broken up and rented out in parts (*appartements*), the occupant of a particular space became more and more a matter of coincidence.[8] Houssin's photograph shows us, metaphorically, this new anonymity of space, which becomes something that exists as an unchanging pattern; it is simply occupied in time by whoever happens to be passing through, without being altered or even affected in the process. So although there is a lot of activity implied here, in a very real sense nothing ever happens. Unceasing action, which has no ability to affect or even forge a relationship with space over time, becomes as static in its implications as the *Rue Daubenton*.

Yet Marville's *Rue Daubenton* did undergo change, as did all of the streets on the path of Haussmann's demolition squad. And this points up a very real difference between Marville's photographs and those of the stereographic photographers like Houssin. Marville was still living in narrative time; by chronicling the changes in space over time, he was giving us a clear, linear sense of history. In the stereographic photographs, on the other hand, there is no possibility for history. These pictures are about instantaneity, a frozen present that gives no clue to a past or a future. Whereas Marville's works separate the "before," "during," and "after" of lived experience, photographs like Houssin's show us only a continuous "during," seen over and over again. This relentless "during" is a stasis, the exact opposite of the activity it purports to express. And it took its toll on the inhabitants of Paris, on those anonymous people in the street, as is nowhere better expressed than in Baudelaire's poem "In Passing," (1860) one of the *Tableaux Parisiens* (Parisian Scenes) in *Les Fleurs du Mal*:

The traffic roared around me, deafening!
Tall, slender, in mourning—noble grief!—
a woman passed, and with a jeweled hand
gathered up her black embroidered hem;
stately yet lithe, as if a statue walked . . .
And trembling like a fool, I drank from eyes
as ashen as the clouds before a gale
the grace that beckons and the joy that kills.

Lightning . . . then darkness! Lovely fugitive
whose glance has brought me back to life! But where
is life—not this side of eternity?
Elsewhere! Too far, too late, or never at all!
Of me you know nothing, I nothing of you—you
whom I might have loved and who knew that too![9]

fig 3.[18]
Anonymous, stereocard, *Rue de Rivoli,* n.d.
(Metropolitan Museum of Art, Gift in memory of Kathleen W. Naef
and Weston J. Naef, Sr., 1982, New York)

fig 3.[19]
Anonymous, stereocard, *Boulevard de Strasbourg,* n.d.
(Metropolitan Museum of Art, Gift in memory of Kathleen W. Naef
and Weston J. Naef, Sr., 1982, New York)

fig 3.²⁰

Anonymous, stereocard, *Pont Neuf,* n.d. (Metropolitan Museum of Art, Gift in Memory of Kathleen W. Naef and Weston J. Naef, Sr., 1982, New York)

fig 3.²¹

Anonymous, stereocard, *Boulevard des Italiens,* n.d. (Metropolitan Museum of Art, Gift in Memory of Kathleen W. Naef and Weston J. Naef, Sr., 1982, New York)

Though caught in the midst of the hustle and bustle of the city, the narrator, like Aunt Phasie, considers himself apart; he rests passively, an isolated voyeur, while "The traffic roar(s) around (him), deafening!" Just as the anonymous crowd was brought to Jacques's sick old aunt, in a thunderous clamor beyond her control, so the traffic on the Parisian streets brings forth a woman whom the narrator "might have loved." She appears, on a wave of movement, and instantly becomes an object of fantasy and desire. Yet just as the crowd brings this woman to the narrator, so inevitably does it bear her away on its inexorable tides. And the fleeting contact, made only with the eyes and the imagination, will never be consummated, will never even have a chance to withstand the test of true human intimacy.

There is an emotional stasis here, a stasis that persists not only in spite of but because of ceaseless activity. For the traffic roars around the narrator—it is the bringer of all things, but the keeper of none. Its movement is inexorable; it deafens the man, and paralyzes not only his ability to love but also his will to act on his desire. Yet set in opposition to this unrelenting movement is the momentary visual exchange that has occurred, which in an instant has transcended time and place and opened up the windows onto another world.

In the contrast between these two types of experience, Baudelaire has created two distinctly different experiences of time that struggle within the context of the poem. The one is the time of physical activity, of the ebb and flow of the city; the other, however, is the time of subjective experience, a different kind of time, a moment of spiritual insight wrested with difficulty out of the incessant march of the metropolis. Once recognized, this illumination became the "joy that kills," for it could only throw into "darkness" the emptiness that had come before it and that would surely follow. For to Baudelaire this was the experience of "life," and it existed only "elsewhere," in opposition to the hustle and bustle of the city streets. The Paris of the 1860s was a place where physical activity had ceased to be the sign of life, where it became, instead, a harbinger of a thoroughly modern type of spiritual and emotional death—a death that could only be recognized in the light of its opposite, that one moment of subjective illumination that could color a lifetime and make one despair for all eternity.

This type of conflict could only afflict a man like Baudelaire's narrator, who perceived himself apart from the crowd, and who noticed, therefore, the losses—of oneself and others—that one sustained in the hurried activity of the new metropolis. The clash of these two distinct temporal experiences on the boulevards of Haussmann's Paris is the sign of his discomfiture; it signals the onset of modernity, and it provides, finally, the clue to what most distinguishes Marville's work from Houssin's. Marville might have been "Haussmann's man," but his work is still a resistance to the history through which he lived, an attempt to transcend its ceaseless march. This photographer, with his long exposure times and his classically balanced compositions, was searching to find the still point in a turning world—a world in which the activity of people must, for the moment, be abolished. In this silence, one could center oneself as one centered the subjects of a photograph; one could take a long, last, lingering look and wrest out of the relentless flow one image to hold, to carry away. Such a possibility did not exist in the Paris created by Houssin and his colleagues; theirs was the modern world of speed and progress, of traffic and circulation, of the collective excitement of the "breathless crowd." In the instantaneity of their eternal present, the popular audience found its metaphor for the Paris of the Industrial Age, the Paris of Haussmann and the Second Empire. And perhaps, by losing themselves in the traffic's thunderous roar, these anonymous promeneurs managed not to notice that Marville's resistance to history, like Baudelaire's romantic love, was to be the "last spark of heroism amid decadence: a declining daystar, glorious, without heat and full of melancholy." [10]

IV

On Camels and Cathedrals

I n around 1860, Henri Le Secq photographed the west facade of the Cathedral of Notre-Dame, the religious and
monumental center of the city of Paris *(fig. 4.¹)*. Using the calotype
process, the paper negative technique invented by William Henry
Fox Talbot and then used to great effect by French photographers
during the 1850s, Le Secq chose a subject which would remain
motionless long enough for his prolonged exposure time and
which, moreover, allowed him to take a picture that fit into the
conventional category of views of cities, monuments, and art
works—a category already popular by the time photography was
invented, but one that became a booming photographic industry.
Le Secq was one of five photographers who had been selected by
the Commission des Monuments Historiques in 1851 to photograph historical monuments and architecture in five provincial
centers of France. As discussed in chapter 2, the negatives and few
prints produced under the auspices of this short-lived program,
entitled the Mission Héliographique, were designed to preserve

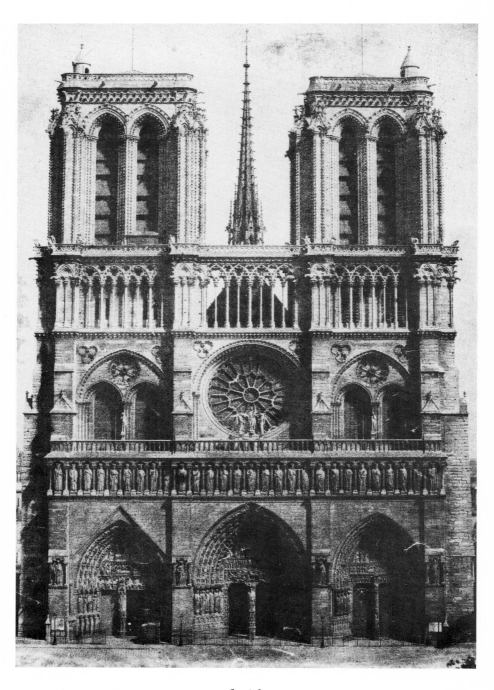

fig 4.[1]

H. Le Secq, *Notre-Dame de Paris,* c. 1860
(Bibliothèque Nationale, Paris)

France's heritage, a heritage that was being threatened not only by decay and industrialization but also by restoration.

The restoration issue—a major concern in Paris in those years—was particularly pertinent to Notre-Dame, since it was the publication of Victor Hugo's *Notre-Dame de Paris* in 1831 that gave rise to restoration fever in the first place. As a consequence of the vogue for the romanticism of ruins, the science of medieval archaeology developed during the 1830s and led to the formation of both the Societé Française d'Archaeologie and the above-mentioned Commission des Monuments Historiques. Hugo treated the dilapidated condition of Notre-Dame as symptomatic of France's negligence of its Gothic architectural heritage, and his book therefore caused a popular outcry of concern that encouraged the government to hire J.-B.-H. Lassus and Eugène-Emmanuel Viollet-le-Duc in 1844 to restore the famous church to the tune of 2,650,000 francs. As is well known, the restoration tactics of these gentlemen—but particularly of the more adventuresome and inventive Viollet-le-Duc, who promised to reconstruct the cathedral in "a complete state such as might never have existed,"[1] and who took total control of the project after Lassus's death—was a major source of controversy in Paris in the 1840s and 1850s. So this venerable edifice, which had long been central to the city's spiritual, social, and geographical life, was once again at center stage when Le Secq approached it for the purpose of preserving it once again: this time in the freeze-frame of a photograph.

The church is, of course, on center stage in this picture too. Le Secq has chosen a point of view that places the cathedral's facade directly in the middle of the picture plane, which is completely dominated by the architecture. Le Secq approached the edifice, if not exactly from ground level, at least from a viewpoint low enough to emphasize its massive structure, its scale that physically dwarfs the promeneur/pilgrim who stands before it. Its spire is directly in the center of the picture; its two towers create a symmetry on either side, which emphasizes the classical balance of the photograph and accentuates the stillness and the iconic quality of the facade, an almost two-dimensional sheet of wall whose beauty lies in the sculptural play of light and shadow upon its surface. Le Secq was standing quite close to the cathedral, in the parvis (or outer sanctuary); he has left little space in the picture for anything else, whether it be the sky or, to the left and right, the closely packed houses that line the streets on either side. There is an absolute hierarchy of attention observed in this photograph: this great monument, this massive physical object, stands as a subject that so dominates its environment that it excludes everything extraneous to it.

Le Secq's point of view on Notre-Dame was not, of course, a new one. Over the centuries, views of the west facade recur frequently in drawings and prints; in fact, it can be said that this particular vantage point was the most conventional manner of representing the church. As yet another such representation of Notre-Dame, Le Secq's picture can stand as a photographic flowering of this tradition—a tradition that was soon to be called into question by the changes in the urban space around the cathedral brought on by Haussmannization.

I

Although Baron Haussmann's transformation of Paris left the cathedral (whose restorations were completed in 1863) intact, it created such upheavals in the urban landscape around it on the Ile de la Cité that the popular and traditional ways of perceiving the cathedral itself underwent massive metamorphoses. One of Haussmann's pet projects was the cleanup of this island, which until the 1850s was crammed with shacks and makeshift shanties, filling every inch of available space abutting the church and housing the poor in one of the worst slums of Paris (see *fig. 4.5*). The prefect, the self-styled "demolition artist" of the capital, leveled these slums, scattering the inhabitants to the outlying areas of the city, and built in their place the blocks of public buildings standing there today.

In the process of restructuring the Ile de la Cité, Haussmann qua-
drupled the size of the parvis of the cathedral. This move to extend the approach
to Notre-Dame—the square in front of the facade that functions as the zero
point from which all road distances in France are measured—did not, however,
originate with Haussmann. As early as 1804, Napoleon I had accomplished a
more minor expansion of the square: a shift in the spatial relationship of the
church and its environment that did not go unremarked by commentators on
city affairs, who were obviously appalled at seeing their cathedral surrounded
by such a vacuum of empty space. In 1837, a man named Schmitt, writing about
the projected demolition of the nearby Hôtel Dieu hospital that dominated the
square and straddled the Seine, summarized his feelings about the inappropri-
ateness of monuments isolated in space: "Our beautiful basilica today represents
a large elephant in the middle of a desert. If one pursues the project of clearing
the whole portion of the Hôtel Dieu that remains on the Cité, the elephant will
no longer be anything but a squatting dromedary."[2] Clearly, Mr. Schmitt's perception of a healthy urban fabric was that it should be full; his *horror vacuii*
demanded that all spaces, even and maybe especially those around public monuments, be filled with people and the physical signs of their life and presence.

Schmitt was evidently not in tune with one of the major structuring
principles of what was to become, under Haussmann, the City of the Industrial
Age. Central to the prefect's plan for the rebuilding of Paris, as discussed in
chapter 2, was the concept of *dégagement*: the isolation of major public monuments in space. Once again, the idea of *dégagement* did not originate with
Haussmann; it shows up much earlier in the writings of Quatremère de Quincy,
which were influential at the end of the Ancien Régime, during the First Empire
and also during the Restoration. De Quincy complained that everywhere the
grand Parisian edifices were "obstructed," and he emphasized the importance of
their spatial disengagement from the urban fabric: "One knows to what extent
the beauty of placement adds to an edifice," he wrote, while emphasizing especially the need to disentangle the Cathedral of Notre-Dame.[3] In fact, it was de
Quincy who influenced Napoleon I's earlier expansion of the parvis. Yet his

ideas reached their full fruition in the *dégagements* of Haussmann—and in a visual approach that left the cathedral looking, from Mr. Schmitt's point of view, like a dromedary squatting in the middle of a desert.

Schmitt's outrageous simile makes one thing abundantly clear: after the aggrandizements of the parvis, it became more difficult to perceive Notre-Dame in the way that Le Secq, and numerous artists before him, had. Le Secq's photograph portrays the edifice as exclusive, as massive, as dominating both its environment and the tiny photographer who stood before it with its imposing physical presence. Given the fact that there was little space on any side of the church before the disentanglements of the nineteenth century, the cathedral always existed in close proximity to either the spectator or the buildings that surrounded it and thus could easily both dwarf and dominate its surroundings by virtue of its comparatively large scale. Once the area in front of the church was cleared, however, this visual hierarchy fell apart. The edifice lost its absolute dominance when perceived in the context of a spatial void that dwarfed it and forced it into the position of being seen, not as a self-contained presence, but as a part of a much larger, and less hierarchical, environmental setting. The primacy of its monumental and self-contained physicality was challenged here—a challenge that could not fail to be noticed by a viewer (or a photographer) who could now perceive the grand edifice with the miniaturizing effects of distant vision.

The effects of distant vision were, in fact, central to Haussmann's urban plan. For the first modern urban planner, as already noted, was not content to let his monuments simply sit in the middle of space; each of his disengaged edifices was to be suitably set, like a jewel, in the crossroads of his networks of boulevards, which functioned as vistas—long-range visual perspectives. But this neoclassical idea begins its metamorphosis in Haussmann's Paris, the city of "the cannonshot boulevard, seemingly without end."[4] Vistas were sometimes lost by a pedestrian ambling down a street three miles long, who perceived as his primary reference only the endless avenues; but then a view might suddenly come into focus, as a monument appeared that would change both its scale and its shape in relation to the distance and the details of the urban environment visible around it.

To put this in another, simpler way: in the Paris of Mr. Schmitt's imagination, when one perceived a camel, one perceived a stable object as a reference point, and this stable object was firmly ensconced in a set of relationships with other stable objects and spaces around it. When perceiving the same camel in Haussmann's Paris, however, one was forced, by the scale and the dynamic physical relationships established, to perceive the spatial void of the desert first, and to perceive the camel *within* that void, as a form that changed depending on one's placement within the larger spatial context. For the Paris of the Industrial Age was a city based not on the primacy of architectural structures but on a network of boulevards that restructured the urban fabric into a set of relationships between solids and voids, forms and spaces, masses and empty places. And this is the paradox of Haussmann's concept of *dégagement:* in principle it was an idea that celebrated the physical separation of monuments, but in actual fact what was accomplished was the reshaping of the urban environment in such a way that those monuments became only one element in a much more closely knit relational unity.

A case in point: François Loyer, in his extraordinary *Paris XIXe Siècle: L'Immeuble et L'Espace Urbain,* points out that when Haussmann and his contemporaries actually built monuments to embellish the new city, they created complex architectural structures whose elements were not stylistically bound together into unified, self-contained forms. Rather, the buildings became comprehensible only when seen at the different levels of perception one would attain while walking through the larger urban fabric, when each part was seen in relation to the aspects of the environment to which it referred. "In effect," Loyer writes, "the will to coherence of the urban form overshadows that of the clarity of the articulation of parts: the city is a whole, indissolubly linked to the point that the monument no longer succeeds in disengaging itself from it." [5] So the purported disengagement of monuments led instead to their more intense engagement with the surrounding environment: to the breakdown in the hierarchical status and concomitant isolation of monumental objects, and the creation of a more democratic unity of spaces, monuments, nonmonumental architecture, and even urban furnishings, which are bound together by the network of the city streets.

And by vision, of course, since this whole picture comes together only in the eye of the beholder. Such an arrangement throws the burden of interpretation of the city onto the spectator, the promeneur. The human experience of the prefect's city was a series of shifting points of view, of vistas—not the unchanging one Haussmann intended, but splinters of vision that together made up the totality of a visual experience that changed depending on where you stood, how you moved, and where you directed your gaze. The only way, in fact, to grasp the unchanging aesthetic order imposed on the capital by Haussmann's plan was by looking at a map or at the bird's-eye views made photographically available when Félix Nadar took the first aerial photographs of Paris in 1858 (see chap. 5). But the average person was not experiencing the city from the sky, and from the ground, the city as a whole—the large city, regional in scope, planned on a scale exceeding the unaided range of human senses—was lost. Paris became instead a series of perspectives: contingent, fragmented, variable, and completely dependent on the subjective mechanism of perception, of sight. The spatial separations built into Haussmann's Paris were, ultimately, built to be bridged by vision. And so, in another paradox inherent in the concept of *dégagement,* these physical distances only served to bring the city closer to the spectator—so close, in fact, that it became an internal phenomena, an endless series of personal perceptions.

II

No medium was better suited to describe these personal perceptions than the new medium of photography. As already discussed, numerous image makers worked—on their own initiative or for a speculative market—to interpret the changing spaces and structures of the city, providing two-dimensional interpretations of Haussmann's three-dimensional urban designs. One popular interpretation was the panoramic view: a photographic vista of the urban environment that well exemplified the subjective, contingent nature of the prefect's Paris.

The word "panorama" was first coined in London around 1792; a neologism piggybacking *pan* (all) and *horama* (to see), it originally referred very specifically to the cylindrical picture between 10 and 20 meters in diameter, 10 and 14 meters in height, and up to 140 meters in length described in Robert Barker's patent of June 19, 1787, for a 360-degree painting called *Nature at a Glance*. The painting was illuminated by daylight, and viewers arrived at a platform in the middle of the canvas by moving through a dark passageway, accessible only after paying an admission fee. Surrounded by the view, spectators were immersed in the experience of "nature at a glance."

Almost simultaneously, though completely independently of one another, the Englishman Lord Hamilton, the German J. A. Breysig, and the American Robert Fulton "invented" this art form of the Industrial Revolution, geared toward the physical standpoint of the viewer, whose roving eye determined the visual experience. Caught from the beginning in the gray areas between high culture and technological invention, between art and commerce, the painted panoramas—like the Montgolfier Brothers' hot air balloons, airborne since 1783—exploded the normal limitations of eighteenth-century human vision by offering up the entire horizon for perusal, in a complete circular view. Panorama paintings also democratized visual imagery by making detailed pictures of places, people, or contemporary and historical events accessible to a broad, paying audience. Seen in communal groups like films and newsreels, these dinosaurs of the mass media satisfied a need for optical information, which was

fig 4.[2]
Anonymous, follower of F. Martens, *Panorama of Paris, the Pont Neuf,*
before 1850 (Musée Carnavalet, Paris)

fig 4.[3]
H. Bayard, *Panorama from the Roof of the Tuileries,* c. 1847
(Société Française de Photographie, Paris)

more efficiently supplied by photography and illustrated newspapers by the mid-nineteenth century, when the large-scale panorama painting craze came to an end.

The word "panorama" changed its meaning during the course of the nineteenth century to include any picture or series of pictures, big or small, that provided an overall view or a survey of its subject. It covered a motley range of images, both popular and otherwise: bird's-eye views, maps and diagrams, painted or photographed depictions encompassing a broad angle of vision, serial or continuous images chronicling a narrative or describing a location or situation. For the first time, this catchall phrase was used to lump together what the philosopher G. W. Liebniz would call the "divine overview" and the variable,

fig 4.[4]

H. Bayard, *Houses and rooftops of Paris, view taken looking toward the windmills of Montmartre,* n.d. (Bibliothèque Historique de la Ville de Paris, Paris)

multiple perceptions of the "monad" in time and space—treating them as two ways of approaching truth.[6] Such a definition allowed plenty of room for both macrocosmic paintings and microcosmic photographic fragments—those contingent "perspectives" that, when seen together, recreated a cumulative, global vision of a given site.

There were perspectives of Paris produced before the invention of photography; the most impressive series remains Israel Silvestre's gravures of the city, done from various points of view (and often including Notre-Dame) during the seventeenth century. The inclusive vistas now known as panoramic made their appearance early in the history of photography, for by the 1840s daguerreotypists like the German Frédéric Martens and his followers had begun producing sweeping surveys of the interlocking fabric of the capital *(fig. 4.²)*. Martens's daguerreotype camera, invented in 1844 and produced commercially by N. P. Lerebours, had a lens that swiveled around a fixed axis; as it moved, the image was recorded through a vertical slit and was formed on a curved plate. Five inches by seventeen-and-a-half inches, these pictures (like all daguerreotypes) are mirror images. Extremely detailed and very rare, since the process itself was excruciatingly difficult, these metal panoramas are echoed by less ambitious paper prints produced by image makers like Hippolyte Bayard *(fig. 4.³, 4.⁴)*, who experimented with views taken from the rooftops of Paris during the early 1840s.

Such views showed up frequently in the albums and exhibitions of the 1850s, and in 1855 the Bisson Brothers won a first-prize medal for works, including panoramas, displayed at the Universal Exposition *(fig. 4.⁵)*. That same year the painter Clausel created a 360-degree photographic panorama composed of twenty-one plates—overlapping images taken in sequence with a normal plate camera.[7] But single-image panoramic imagery became an important part of the popular mainstream only in the 1860s—at just the time when Haussmann's *travaux* were making their greatest impact on the face, and the life, of the city.

These photographic panoramas were overviews, often taken from above-ground vantage points, that focused not on isolated or particular parts of

fig 4.[5]

Bisson Brothers, *Panorama of Paris taken from the towers of Notre-Dame Cathedral,* n.d. (early 1850s) (Bibliothèque Nationale, Paris)

fig 4.[6]

E. Baldus, *Arc de l'Etoile,* n.d. (Bibliothèque Nationale, Paris)

fig 4.[7]

Anonymous, *The Pantheon,* published in Blanquart-Evrard (editor),
Paris Photographique, 1851–1853 (Bibliothèque Nationale, Paris)

fig 4.[8]
C. Soulier, *Panorama of Paris from the Colonnade of the Louvre,* before 1867
(Bibliothèque Nationale, Paris)

fig 4.[9]

C. Soulier, *Panorama of Paris*, n.d. (Bibliothèque Nationale, Paris)

fig 4.[10]

E. Baldus, *Panorama de la Cité*, 1864 (Bibliothèque Nationale, Paris)

the city (buildings, monuments etc., as seen in *figs. 4.⁶, 4.⁷*) but on the spectacle of the urban environment as seen from a specific point of view. From the vantage point of the beholder—in this case the photographer—the viewer sees the non-hierarchical sweep of the urban fabric: the objects and spaces, monuments and streets, residences and parks, and the relationships between them that together comprised the City of Light. The popularity of panoramas (including those by Charles Soulier, *figs. 4.⁸*, and *4.⁹*, whose studio specialized in this type of work) during the 1860s was understandable, for these views were the quintessential Haussmannian perspectives. The city became a perspective, a contingent view strictly dependent on the time and space of the beholder, a "slice of life" that implied something much larger. That "something larger" can be seen here, surrounding the Cathedral of Notre-Dame de Paris, in Baldus's panoramic photograph of the Ile de la Cité, produced in 1864 *(fig. 4.¹⁰)*.

I I I

When taking this photograph, Baldus was standing on the Right Bank, in an atelier in the Louvre (whose reconstruction, and union with the Tuileries, he documented extensively for the government in the mid-1850s, as discussed in chapter 2). As in Le Secq's photograph, Notre-Dame is centered here—but only as a small form in the background, surrounded by the clusters of buildings on the Ile de la Cité and encircled by the rivers and bridges that connect it to the rest of the city life. Like all panoramic photographers, Baldus did not focus on any object that could provide a hierarchy of attention but instead depicted the relationships between monuments, landmarks, buildings, and landscape elements. The high vantage point allowed the photographer to better grasp the sweep of these relationships, to perceive the ensemble without differences in height blocking his view. So the picture is divided roughly in half: the top half is the sky, and the bottom half is completely filled by the river and the built structures of the human-made environment.

This is an extremely stable, horizontal pictorial arrangement. But in the context of the bottom half of the photograph, two distinct and even contrasting formal constructs work together. The Ile de la Cité, centered within the image, is a solid, stable circular mass whose pictorial interest is created by the diversified details of its architecture. That mass is, however, contrasted by the river flowing to the left of the island in a diagonal line, from the bottom right to the middle left ground of the photograph; this sweep is reinforced by the forms of the boats (the public baths) parked near the banks and echoed by the quai itself. So the picture is a complicated combination of masses and lines, of still forms and active ones, of nature and culture, of buildings and spaces, that together make a complex statement about Paris: for the city here seems to swirl around the Ile de la Cité in general, and Notre-Dame in particular. Baldus has played down the physical form of Notre-Dame, but he has, in the process, emphasized the church's role as the pivotal stable point of something much larger than itself—the city's life.

So, in essence, Baldus is making a statement similar to the one made by Le Secq about the importance of the cathedral, though his statement reflects, in its form, the different concepts of monuments, and of their place in the totality of the built environment, made manifest by Haussmannization. And it is that change in form that is crucial here, for it describes a change in perception as radical as the changes in the map of Paris. Le Secq's cathedral is a timeless, eternal one; disengaged from its context, centered and dominant within the image, with the iconic stillness of a Byzantine icon, his church is independent of time and space, of change and death. Baldus's Notre-Dame, on the other hand, is totally engaged with the rest of the city, and with the photographer; existing only as a point of view, it is intimately bound to its image maker for its form and meaning. Baldus's panorama, and thus his cathedral, can only exist within the time and space of the city and of the beholder. It is a fragment of vision, a fleeting perception, contingent always on the subjective spectator who took the photograph and thus gave it life—or rather, this particular interpretation of its life, an interpretation that can shift in space, if one moves a few steps this way or that, or in time, by a change in light. Baldus's Notre-Dame has stepped down from the heavens and will now take its chances in the historical world, the world where cities themselves are demolished and rebuilt. In that world it will be, of necessity, more fragile, but it will also participate in the urban life around it in a way that had never been possible before.

V

Souvenirs

Paris, Empire des Morts

D uring the 1850s and 1860s, it became a literary platitude to describe Paris as a dying city. This perception of decay existed as early as 1830, when the historian Friedrich von Raumer wrote in his letters: "Yesterday I surveyed the enormous city from the Notre-Dame tower. Who built the first house, when will the last one collapse and the ground of Paris look like the ground of Thebes and Babylon?"[1] The broad overview from the tower of Notre-Dame—the bird's-eye view so characteristic of the nineteenth century because of the Montgolfier brothers' invention of ballooning in 1783—seemed to encourage sweeping meditations on the city not only in space but also in time.

The idea that Paris was to die like the cities of antiquity, that it too had a cycle of creation and destruction, infused Victor Hugo's poetic cycle "A l'Arc de Triomphe," for instance.[2] It was seminal to the poetry of Baudelaire and gave Maxime Du Camp the impetus and inspiration to write his massive, six-volume survey of the city administration.[3] As Paul Bouget explained, describing Du Camp's epiphany in 1862 while waiting for his new eyeglasses near the optician's shop near the Pont Neuf: "The slight deterioration of his eyesight . . . reminded him of the law of the inevitable infirmity of all human things. . . . It suddenly occurred to the man who had travelled widely in the Orient, who was acquainted with the deserts whose sand is the dust of the dead, that this city, too, whose bustle was all around him, would have to die some day, the way so many capitols had died." Du Camp's resolution, at that moment, "to write the kind of book about Paris that the historians of antiquity failed to write about their cities"[4] was his attempt to preserve Paris before it slipped into the stream of time—an end that suddenly appeared not only inevitable but imminent.

This was not simply a Romantic literary conceit. When, in 1856, Théophile Gautier published an essay about Paris entitled "Mosaique des Ruines,"[5] and when, in 1867, Edmond About's article "Dans Les Ruines" appeared,[6] no one in the city would have had any trouble understanding their references. For the generation living in the age of Georges-Eugène Haussmann, a city in ruins was part of the day-to-day reality of their lives *(fig. 5.¹)*. For Parisians watching the rubble of their past being swept away by the onset of a new administratively conceived and realized social order, death was in the air.

Those living with the discomforts of the soul brought on by such an upheaval, however, defined the death of Paris in a very specific way. Obviously, the city had suffered no physical or literal death. It was, indeed, to an outside observer, in much better shape after Haussmann than before. As quoted earlier, Maxime Du Camp himself said that "in 1848, Paris was about to become uninhabitable"[8] and admitted that the reconstruction could only be said to have "given to Paris facilities of communication and cleanliness that it hadn't formerly known."[9] Many of the disease-ridden slum areas were destroyed, while a large number of the city's poor had been shunted to the outlying areas, some of which had been annexed in 1859 with the geographical expansion of the city limits. Wide, tree-lined boulevards efficiently handled the traffic and overcrowd-

fig 5.[1]

P. Edmonds, *Tour Bon Bec*, taken during the restoration of the Conciergerie, Paris, late 1850s (Musée Carnavalet, Paris)

ing that had almost choked the Paris of 1848. Commerce and trading were brisk, in shops on the new streets as well as in the first department stores. In addition, there were functional sewers, parks, new monuments, and squares; the city finally had a reasonable water supply, gaslights, better security, and easy access to trains. By all the statistics, and all the signs of activity, Paris during and after Haussmann was a boom town, not a graveyard.

So the mourners were reacting to something else, something that could not be measured by all these signs of civic amelioration. The death they perceived was of a more metaphysical order, that state characterized by Walter Benjamin as a "sadness about what was and lack of hope for what is to come." [10] This sense of loss is perhaps best expressed in an essay by Louis Blanc entitled "Le Vieux Paris," published in 1867.[11] In the article, Blanc quotes a number of famous historical personages who describe their adoration of Paris. The author then goes on to point out that the city they loved was crowded, dirty, and ill-kept; that many of its most famous landmarks—its grand hotels, boulevards, and bustling cafés—did not yet exist and could not have been the reason for these great men's affection. He concludes, therefore, that "in all the periods of its existence, Paris has had a charm independent of its exterior beauty." [12]

Blanc locates the source of this irresistible charm in the "great men and great things" [13] that, by contributing to the ongoing intellectual life of Paris, had left their historic imprint in the physical environment: an imprint that could be perceived, indeed imbibed, by later generations. When he quotes Goethe extolling the virtues of "this universal city, where each step on a bridge, on a *place* brings to mind a great past, where at each corner of a street a fragment of history unfolds," [14] he is pointing out that the spiritual life of a city is dependent on the "illustrious phantoms" [15] that have infused its physical form with their being, with the "images that animate each of the (old) stones." [16] And Blanc goes on to say that "it is this which constitutes what I would willingly call (Paris's) soul; because cities have a soul, which is their past; and their material beauty only has value when it lets subsist the visible traces of this other beauty which is comprised of memories." [17]

Blanc was, in other words, equating the soul of a city with its history, as it has inscribed itself in matter over time. To him, the physical and the spiritual were inseparable, so the retention of the city's memory was a question of landmark preservation. From this point of view, the concepts of urban death that took shape during the Second Empire become very clear because Haussmann, by demolishing the old, did nothing less than separate the body of Paris from its soul. The prefect destroyed much more than objects and spaces—he destroyed the repositories of mental images, demolished the histories and meanings of places that together shaped the collective memory. He created a rupture with the past, with tradition, with metaphorical thought that was irreparable, and he left the "illustrious phantoms" of memory wandering homeless through the new metropolis.

The resultant schism between image and object, spirit and matter, memory and experience might explain, in part, why it was in the Paris of the Second Empire that photography first became a socially functional medium of expression.[18] The foundations of our own mass-media society were laid during this period when, to quote Joseph Joubert, artists became "more inspired by the image than by the actual presence of objects."[19] The illustrious phantoms of the past were at large, and it became photography's business to find them, to capture the images that still animated the old stones that had not yet been demolished or dispersed. As discussed throughout this book, much of the photographic work produced by artists as diverse as Charles Marville and the members of the Mission Héliographique during the Second Empire was literally involved with preservation of old monuments, buildings, and streets. But there is another, more abstract way in which the medium, which immediately transforms the present into history, reflected the turning backward, toward the past, that characterized many of the thinkers and artists of the age. For a photograph, like the Paris that they perceived, is (to quote Roland Barthes) "without future." Barthes's contention, discussed at length in chapter 1, is that the advent of photography divided the history of the world; suddenly, because of its visual traces, the past became as certain as the present. But the image that photography captures from history does not, as we do, swim on in time; "motionless, the photograph flows back from presentation to retention." [20]

And this is, of course, one of the ironies of the Age of Progress. Among its greatest technical and scientific advances was a medium that looked not forward but backward. Photography was a still point, a brake in history's ceaseless march. But it reflected the experience of many Parisians in another, more critical way — for it, like Haussmannization, created a rupture in the flow of time, an unbridgeable gap between memory and experience, an irreparable breach between the *this has been* and the *this is*.

But what about the flesh-and-blood people who lived in this Paris, a Paris that existed geographically and historically in real time and space? For many of the artists and writers working during the Second Empire, active in their own culture and yet still living in memories that failed to match up with the new Paris of their day-to-day experience, life resembled Marcel's experience in Proust's *A la Recherche du Temps Perdu*: a series of snapshots isolated in time that gave contradictory evidence, as if time itself were playing tricks with any concept of truth that appeared to be stable. [21] Those who suffered from this malaise often described themselves, interestingly enough, as "travelers." The Goncourts, in their journal of November 1860, stated that the changes in Parisian life "make me feel, in this country so dear to my heart, like a traveler. I am a stranger to what is coming, to what is, as I am to these new boulevards." [22] And Nadar, the subject of this study, put it this way: "Where is my infancy, where my youth, where all the aspects that bring back to me fond memories, where have I finally left all that is for us the Patrimony, I am like a traveller who arrived yesterday in a strange city." [23]

Yet none of these men had made any journey in space. Theirs was time travel. Ambiguous, nonphysical, allusive, these time displacements were on certain levels just like capital: fluid, abstract, and invisible. They nonetheless provided the basis for some of the most important changes in this most empirical and positivist of eras. No wonder that, when the Goncourts were attempting to personify the changes in their city, they contrasted the "man about town" twenty years before—an artist, a senior civil servant, an officer, a bourgeois, or a sporting gentleman—with his Second Empire counterpart, who "is almost always a stock-exchange speculator or photographer:" the two equated, as T. J. Clark sees it, because they are both "servants of illusion." [24]

Memories

One of the Second Empire's quintessential "servants of illusion" was Nadar, born Gaspard-Félix Tournachon in 1820. Eighteen years old when his father, a printer, died, Nadar paid his own way as a journalist, a caricaturist, a political activist, a novelist, a photographer, a balloonist, and a prophet of aviation throughout his long life, which ended where it had begun, in Paris, in 1910. His biography, which deserves to be much better known, reads like a checklist of many of the major currents of thought and action in the nineteenth century. Writing in his journals, Baudelaire commented jealously that "Nadar is the most astounding example of vitality," [25] and the photographer himself estimated in 1865 that he knew about 10,000 people in Paris alone. [26] At times it seems inevitable that such unbridled human energy should have produced what is today regarded as one of the most important photographic records of Parisians during the Second Empire, and indeed it is for his portraits of writers, artists, actors, politicians, and cultural figures, all of them his friends, that Nadar is probably most widely recognized.

But he also left us another, much less well known, body of photographs: his pictures of Paris, viewed from both the air and from underground. These were the first photographs ever taken with artificial light or from a balloon, and the technical inventiveness involved was formidable. The photographs themselves are straightforward documents of the sewers and catacombs as well as of the streets and monuments as seen from above, but the real fascination of these works lies in the sheer radicalism of the vision that conceived and executed them.

Describing him as a photo-detective, Walter Benjamin asserted that "Nadar's lead over his professional colleagues was demonstrated when he embarked on taking pictures in the Paris sewers. Thus for the first time discoveries were required of the lens."[27]

In his politics, his friends, his inventions, and his vision, Nadar was consistently and self-consciously a prophet, glorying in both the new media and the new technical experiments that, he felt, were to change the world. This was a man who, more than any other photographer of his time, gloried in modernity and set his sights toward the future. Yet the oeuvre of Nadar is marked by a profound ambivalence toward the modern world of progress in which he lived and which he helped bring into being. Marshall Berman has written: "To be modern is to live a life of paradox and contradiction. . . . We might even say that to be fully modern is to be anti-modern: from Marx's and Dostoevsky's time to our own, it has been impossible to grasp and embrace the modern world's potentialities without loathing and fighting against some of its most palpable realities."[28] It is in this respect, in the paradoxes and contradictions that underlie his attitudes and accomplishments, that Nadar is most "fully modern," and the importance of this ambivalence can best be grasped if one looks at his photographic work as a whole.

A full understanding of the above- and below-ground pictures can only be had by seeing them in the light of the justifiably famous studio portraits—likenesses of such spirits of the age as Baudelaire, Manet, Courbet, Delacroix, George Sand, and Sarah Bernhardt *(figs. 5.², 5.³)*. Much has been said about these works, which often show their sitters in a two-thirds view against a plain backdrop, so I will not treat these pictures in depth here. What does interest me in this regard is the quality of "life"—not only spontaneity and intimacy but of individual character—that is universally accepted, by writers as diverse as Nigel Gosling and André Jammes, as the hallmark of these portraits.[29] Nadar himself summed up his aims on this subject in a statement that served as evidence in a lawsuit against his brother in 1856:

fig 5.[2]

Nadar, *Charles Baudelaire*, 1855 (Bibliothèque Nationale, Paris)

fig 5.3
Nadar, *Sarah Bernhardt*, c. 1866 (Bibliothèque Nationale, Paris)

The theory of photography can be learnt in an hour and the elements of practicing it in a day. . . . What cannot be learnt is the sense of light, an artistic feeling for the effects of varying luminosity and combinations of it, the application of this or that effect to the features which confront the artist in you. What can be learnt even less is the moral grasp of the subject — that instant understanding which puts you in touch with the model, helps you to sum him up, guides you to his habits, his ideas and his character and enables you to produce, not an indifferent reproduction, a matter of routine or accident such as any laboratory assistant could achieve, but a really convincing and sympathetic likeness, an intimate portrait.[30]

Nadar's goal, in other words, was to "sum (his sitter) up," to grasp the essence of "his habits, his ideas and his character" as they revealed themselves in time and light. For Nadar, as for Louis Blanc, the physical and the spiritual were inseparable: the physical appearance, perceived rightly, was itself the revelation of spiritual character. There is a double layer of time here too, a presumption that there is an underlying character that is unchanging, yet that reveals itself in the moment. As a photographer, Nadar was searching for what Baudelaire perceived in Constantin Guys when he wrote, in his essay "The Painter of Modern Life," that "he is the painter of the passing moment and of all the suggestions of eternity that it contains."[31]

This need to blend the ephemeral and the eternal, to reveal not only likeness but also character, might partially explain why, according to Nigel Gosling, Nadar "rarely accepted commissions for the ever-popular deathbed pictures."[32] There are exceptions, though not many, to this rule: the poet Mme. Desbordes-Valmores and the writer Victor Hugo *(fig. 5.⁴)* were two of them. The unity of the physical and spiritual is lacking in a deathbed photograph, even of one's friends; there is only a static likeness, without the moral connotations of character revelation in time that Nadar saw as the raison d'être of his portraiture. Unchanging, immobilized, permanently frozen, a dead body is only physical form—corporeal appearance without the spirit.

fig 5.⁴

Nadar, *Victor Hugo on his Deathbed*, 1885 (Bibliothèque Nationale, Paris)

It stands to reason that such portraits were wildly popular in Hauss-mann's Paris, the beautiful city without a soul. In an increasingly secular society, as Walter Benjamin has commented, "the cult of remembrance of loved ones, absent or dead, offer(ed) a last refuge for the cult value of the picture."[33] These photographs had (as in some parts of the world they still do) an undeniable importance in the death rite, and the playing-out of this role was one of the first and most widespread uses of the medium—especially in photography's very early days, when long exposure times made it difficult to capture the likeness of an animated being. The deathbed picture was one of the nineteenth-century's major contributions to memory, a memory that had increasingly lost its home in the physical environment. Perceived as a nexus point linking the *this has been* with the *this is,* the genre quickly ramifies in meaning beyond any merely private attempt to hold on to what has been lost, so that the impulse to create a memory image from a body devoid of life comes to reflect in microcosm the Second Empire's cultural attitudes toward death and the dead—attitudes that in the preceding years had undergone massive transformations.

The modern cult of death and the dead found its definitive form during the era of Haussmann. As Philippe Ariès has commented, the rituals of mortality have become so completely naturalized in our society that we have forgotten their comparatively recent origins.[34] Throughout the Middle Ages, and to some extent during the sixteenth and seventeenth centuries, the attitude of the living toward the dead was primarily one of indifference. The medieval practice of church-ground burial within the city ensured that the body was *ad sanctos,* as close as possible to the tombs of the saints and contained within a sacred space that would presumably maintain its protection. Beyond this basic precaution, however, the fate of the body itself was deemed of little importance. Besides the rich, who could be buried in personal sepulchres if they chose, most people were interred in unmarked common graves more or less close to the saint's relics depending on the means of the deceased; periodically, when these graves were full and more space was needed, the soil was dug up, and the bones piled helter-skelter in *charniers* (charnels) or the attics of the church. In other words, once buried, the sanctity of the individual body was not of particular concern: no one knew where loved ones' bones were, and no one cared.

This attitude, essentially unchanged for centuries, underwent massive convulsions over the course of the late 1700s through the mid-1850s. First manifesting itself as horror at the idea of decomposing corpses buried in the middle of the city, this cultural shift from indifference to revulsion soon prompted an emblematic shift in practice. Beginning in the 1780s, old cemeteries within the Paris city limits were closed, the bones found in the soil were moved to the newly opened catacombs, and new cemeteries like Père-Lachaise (then on the outskirts of the city) were founded. The administrative government in Paris continued the same policy until the commencement of the Third Republic, and laws on the deposition of the dead were always designed to keep them outside the realm of the living. But during the Second Empire, there was a remarkable and total change in the public opinion on this subject—a change that resulted in one of Haussmann's most resounding urban planning defeats. The prefect had decided to cease inhumations in the famous cemetery of Père-Lachaise, by that time within city limits, and to open a large burial ground in Méry-sur-Oise, a location far enough away from Paris to insure that the capital would never expand around it. He proposed that a special railroad be built to this cemetery, so that all burials would take place by rail, on a train maintained solely for that purpose.

The public was outraged, and the outcry against this plan was immediate. The arguments put forth by the plan's detractors are telling, indeed, of new attitudes toward both death and memory. The leaders of the opposition to the new cemetery, interestingly enough, called themselves the "positivists"—but in this instance positivism represented not only an isolated, avant-garde philosophic position but a merger of the opinions of philosophers and the populace. A statement of May 29, 1881 (signed by M. Lafitte, Director of Positivism, as well as M. Magnin, a mechanic worker, and M. Bernard, an accountant) represented the opinion of the positivist group, fighting to keep the remains of their loved ones near them: "The cult of the dead, thus the establishment of tombs and places of sepulchre that alone really characterizes it, are part of the mother institutions belonging to all civilized populations; it is necessary to admit as a fundamental political principle that the cemetery, no less than the common house, the school or the temple, is one of the integral elements of families and municipalities, and one cannot in consequence have cities without cemeteries." [35] The ideas of Auguste Comte were also in evidence in the book *Paris Without Cemeteries* by a Dr. Robinet, which appeared in 1869. The book called for well-marked tombs that could be visited by survivors and argued that the cult of the dead is a "constitutive element of the human order" and "a spontaneous link of the generations for the society as it is for the family." And, according to Robinet, the link was to *memory:* "Man prolongs beyond death those who have succumbed before him. . . . He institutes for their memory a cult where his heart and spirit strive to assure them perpetuity." [36]

In the same culture that ruptured the *this has been* and the *this is* of the city, memory became the only glue that could hold civilization together. Individual, well-marked tombs, like photographs, became the means to "assure the perpetuity" of people and thus the continuity of the species. The "cult of tombs" was originally conceived during the French Revolution as a way to transform the religious feelings associated with death into secular ones. [37] By the time of Haussmann, the tradition of burying the dead in individual sepulchres that were to be visited by loved ones was well established as a cultural ideal (if not always an affordable reality).

The dead body, in other words, was no longer simply a worn-out vessel once used by the spirit of a person long gone; it in itself was the repository of memory. As Ariès states: "The modern cult of the dead is a cult of memory attached to the body, to the corporeal appearance." [38] Charles Kunstler goes so far as to say that in the eyes of the faithful, remains were as precious as if they were the person himself. [39] The lines between life and death were, evidently, becoming increasingly blurred if a dead body, like a dead city, could live on in memory long after its spirit was gone. Like the discarded stones of old Paris, corpses were once the homes of "illustrious phantoms," and the demands for continuity focused on them as the only bridge between the past and the present. When the spirit was evicted from the environment in the Industrial Age, it took up residence in the memorials to "great men and great things" that were once alive — memorials as permanent as marble markers or as transient as photographs on pieces of paper, which can whither and crumble in time.

Chapter V

Miasma

It may initially seem paradoxical that this death-in-life should be a major theme in the work of a man known, during the Second Empire, as the paragon of vitality—a man who indeed outlived all his contemporaries. Of course, the very fact that Nadar, as a portrait photographer, immobilized the images of the living, taking them out of the flow of time, automatically puts him in the mainstream of the cult of remembrance and retention. But by refusing to cater to the vogue for deathbed pictures, this photographer made it explicit that he, for one, did not confuse the remains of a man with the man himself. His particular understanding of death-in-life during the Second Empire, an understanding he shared with many avant-garde artists if not with the populace, is most evident in the three experimental series he did around Paris: the pictures of the catacombs, the documentary records of the sewers, and the aerial photographs of the city. When this man who was friends with everyone left his studio to work, he never photographed the life of his native city—its social events, its hustle and bustle, its commerce and recreation—even though such explorations were well within photography's technical reach during the 1860s, as the instantaneous views by Adolphe Braun and the stereographic street photographers already discussed make clear. Rather, Nadar chose projects that by definition excluded people. Devoid of human subjects or activity, all of his Paris pictures are, in Victor Hugo's words, about "reality and disappearance."[40]

In a sense, however, Nadar's photographic journeys underground and in the air, undertaken within a three-year period from 1858 to 1861, were also time travels, voyages simultaneously exploring the past and the present of his native city in search of an elusive link. The photographs were, obviously, records of the then-present; they were taken at a particular historical moment and, unlike many of his colleagues such as Henri Le Secq and Charles Nègre, Nadar used his camera to document that moment rather than to express his nostalgia or preservationist instincts. He never sought out old stones or corners filled with the past; it was not his style to make a memory image out of a body devoid of life. He plunged, instead, right into the middle of Haussmann's work, focusing on areas, especially in the sewer and aerial pictures, that were most characteristic of innovative nineteenth-century urban planning. But in using his camera this way, Nadar found himself caught between the city he lived in and the city he loved and remembered—and in the conflict between the image in his mind and the image on the photographic plate, a time displacement of massive proportions occurred.

This disjunction is not particularly evident in the photographs themselves. Nadar himself spells it out clearly in his little known essay, "Le Dessus et le dessous de Paris" ("The Above and Below of Paris"), which was published in *Paris-Guide.* According to Jean Prinet and Antoinette Dilasser, the artist, when he began his underground series in 1861, had already promised his above- and below-ground pictures, as well as an accompanying article, to Louis Ulbach for a book scheduled to appear in 1867, in time for the Universal Exposition in Paris.[41] Taking images and text together then, in the fashion intended by the artist, one gains a double insight into exactly how Nadar was viewing Paris, both through his eyes and through his mind. And what thus stands revealed is the yawning chasm that apparently separated sight and sensibility for those unfortunate souls suffering from the malaise brought on by Haussmann's transformation of the city.

Any discussion of Nadar's vision of death-in-life should, of course, begin with his pictures of the catacombs. Before he could venture underground with his camera, he had to perfect the artificial light processes with which he began experimenting in 1858. He invented a system of lights and reflectors using Bunsen batteries for which he registered a patent on February 4, 1861.[42] These technical experiments must be seen, by the way, in the context of a photographic community within which the lines between art, science, invention, and commercialism were not yet clearly drawn. Nadar had no formal art training; but many of his colleagues during the 1850s were painters who exhibited in the juried art Salon and who nevertheless produced all manner of photographs—for expressive as well as technical or commercial purposes—as a way of exploring and

expanding the vocabulary of the new visual medium. In the openness of its possibilities, the decade of the 1850s was indeed a golden age of photography, and
Nadar's experiments took place in an environment where all explorations, of
whatever sort, immediately became part of the ongoing dialogue.

Nadar perfected his artificial light arrangements by first taking portraits
of his friends at night in his studio. Shortly thereafter, with the support of city
officials (to whom he gave two sets of the finished photographs), he descended
into the depths. The work was arduous and by his accounts often frustrating.
He visited first the sewers and then (using magnesium light instead of Bunsen
batteries) the catacombs. He emerged, after three months underground, with a
hundred pictures and the comment that he wouldn't wish such work even on his
worst enemy.[43]

In order to understand Nadar's attraction to such a project, it is important to recognize the horrific image of subterranean Paris that had persisted
unchanged in the collective imagination since the late eighteenth century. By
Nadar's time, the reality of underground Paris had diverged radically from this
image, but, as Baudelaire knew so well, "no human heart/changes half so fast
as a city's face."[44] The best testament to the persistence of the old, fearful image
into the Second Empire was Jean Valjean's terrifying trek through the sewers in
Les Misérables, published in 1862.[45]

In this, his best known novel, Victor Hugo compared the underbelly of
Paris to a vast sponge, full of holes left by the stones with which the city itself
had been built.[46] Over the centuries, many of the old quarries had been overused
or neglected, and by the 1770s Parisians became nervous that the ground under
them was on the verge of collapse. Their terror was only confirmed by several
appalling incidents, including one in 1778 when a fault opened, the ground
caved in, and seven people disappeared.[47] This fear of the depths was exacer-
bated by the occasional ravages of the inadequate and faulty sewer system,
nicknamed "The Stink-Hole."[48] Unexplored and uncontrollable, this site of un-
imaginable horrors lived up to its reputation in 1802, when it flooded to such
an extent that its mire spread over Paris from the Champs-Elysées to the Place

des Victoires to the Rue de la Roquette. Probably the most terrifying manifesta-
tion of the "revolution" in the bowels of the earth, however, was the spontaneous exhumation of the dead who, over centuries, had been buried in the
Cemetery of the Innocents, in the center of the city. The common graves were
too crowded, and the turnover was so rapid that the bodies had no chance to
decompose. Finally, one day in 1780, the pressure from the walls of a mass grave
caused the walls of a basement adjacent to the putrid cemetery to burst—and
as a result hundreds of corpses in various states of decomposition spilled into
someone's house.[49]

It was this particular incident that ultimately led to the closing of the
Cemetery of the Innocents and other burial grounds within the city, and thus to
the opening in 1786 of the catacombs in an old quarry near Mont-Rouge, then
outside of the city limits. Richard Etlin has called the catacombs the "only real-
ization of a sublime landscape" in Paris,[50] and it is clear that Nadar saw his
descent into their depths as a Dantesque plunge. "We are going to penetrate, to
reveal the arcana of the most profound and secret caverns," he wrote.[51] In his
fascination with death and debris, as well as in his compulsion to explore a
landscape whose very function was to subsume all traces of individuality within
a great nothingness, Nadar was, of course, a Romantic: he set himself in tireless
pursuit of a sublime shiver in a realm where none of the reference points of
normal life applied.

In the catacombs, the entire premise underlying both the deathbed photograph and the cult of tombs was immediately negated. There, neither physical
appearance nor historical accomplishment could preserve the individuality of
the dead; quite the contrary—it was the nature of the Catacombs to throw randomly together the bones of kings and criminals, philosophers and paupers, in
the "confused equality of Death."[52] Nadar's essay "Le Dessus et le dessous de
Paris" is full of comments about the bones and skulls that had been detached
from their bodies and dispersed, about the people who "had loved, had been
loved," and who were now an unrecognizable pile of silent debris "without
name, forgotten, lost." Even memory itself, he remarked, had been obliterated

in this place "where all comes to vanish, even the memory of the father in the son." Six million Parisian lives had ended there in oblivion and ruin. Indeed, a few of Nadar's pictures suggest the weary melancholy of memento mori; particularly eloquent are the pictures that show skulls and bones lying heaped or randomly scattered in the recesses of dark, mysterious caves.

Among the latter is the image in which a skull and several bones, small and isolated, sit on the ground of a cavern steeped in shadows *(fig. 5.5)*. This nature morte is almost centered, and it is highlighted by Nadar's artificial light. But such dramatic treatment only emphasizes the insignificance of these tiny human remains, detritus that seems to float in the void of darkness dominating the photograph. Most of the picture plane is empty space, so the formal construction of the image is defined not by objects but by the patterns of light and darkness that encircle the soil and stones of the cave. The light might illuminate a skull or reveal, on the left and in the background, a lettered sign or some other vestige of human life. But it is clear also that this light is transitory and weak, soon to be swallowed by the shadows.

In this picture, the "sublime landscape" of which Etlin spoke is very much in evidence, and to that degree the image is anomalous, atypical of the series. For however tenaciously the collective imagination clung to its Romantic vision, the catacombs were themselves a pure product of the Industrial Age. As with the rest of Haussmann's Paris, the ideal of planning was dominant, so that even the sublime was orderly; even the void had roads, signs, and direction. At first the catacombs consisted of nothing more than piles of bones, but beginning in 1810 the city government decided to strengthen the caverns and replace this haphazard arrangement with a new, nineteenth-century kind of order: an order of walls and crossroads, of monuments and geometric designs. Construction at the site was, at the time of Nadar's visit, in full swing as a result of the recent exhumation and transfer of large quantities of bones; the photographer even captured a wall of bones half built, a Second Empire work-in-progress.

The twelve workers assigned to the catacombs were responsible for structuring the dispersed skeletal parts into neat walls that, enlivened by decora-

fig 5.[5]

Nadar, *The Catacombs,* 1861 (Bibliothèque Nationale, Paris)

fig 5.[6]
Nadar, *The Catacombs,* 1861 (Bibliothèque Nationale, Paris)

fig 5.[7]
Nadar, *The Catacombs*, 1861 (Bibliothèque Nationale, Paris)

tive lines of skulls, were euphemistically called "facades." The skulls that composed the decorative designs were chosen, not because of any historical or personal significance, but only because of their state of conservation. Devoid of any living significance, they became, as it were, "art for art's sake." And, as Nadar reported with more than a hint of irony, management was satisfied that these constructions "made the aspect (of the caverns) interesting, almost agreeable." (So agreeable, in fact, that in 1874 they were definitively opened to the public as a tourist attraction, though visits had been allowed, on and off, since the days of Napoleon.)

It is this orderly, constructed aspect of the catacombs—the aspect most visible during the Second Empire—that Nadar documented in most of his pictures. The photographs focus on the pathways and the walls of the caves; he often recorded the crossroads where two walls, with their diverse patterns and decorations, meet. This vantage point was chosen, for example, in one picture that, despite its subject matter, has lost all vestiges of the sublime landscape discussed earlier *(fig. 5.⁶)*. In this particular image, culture has triumphed over the ravages of nature. Though darkness is a major element in almost all of the catacomb pictures, here the light is stronger than in the picture discussed above, and it is focused on the walls of bones that, with their solidity and decorative embellishments, dominate the photograph. No longer tiny and scattered, the remains have become a human mass, though one divorced from any individualized human context or macabre association. Instead, the bones have become building blocks in a larger, supra-personal construction, abstract in its geometric design. The ground soil is neatly organized and clean here, free of unwanted detritus, and Nadar's choice of vantage point emphasizes the efficiency of these crossroads as places of exchange—checkpoints in the orderly circulation of traffic, alive and otherwise, that flowed through these once uncharted and mysterious caves.

This emphasis on movement and dynamism was appropriate, since Nadar also documented the markers that described the origins of various groups of bones and the date when they had been brought to the caves. For Nadar, as we have seen, the transfer of bones was a contemporary issue, not a historical one, and with the increasing number of cemetery closures throughout the nineteenth century, funeral cortèges carrying remains to their new resting place became a familiar sight. Nadar himself was aware of the specific transfers that took place in 1859 and 1860—the same period that the cult of tombs was reaching its apogee. It is, of course, one of the paradoxes of death in nineteenth-century Paris that while prevailing wisdom insisted upon the new garden cemeteries like Père-Lachaise, where the deceased could rest peacefully and permanently in their own sepulchres, the bones of millions of former Parisians were in transit through the city streets. Small wonder that Nadar, writing about the catacombs, came to the conclusion that "even death itself doesn't guarantee us protection against expropriation."

It seems that, in Haussmann's Paris, the empire of the dead and the empire of the living obeyed similar laws: real estate evictions affected city residents, "illustrious phantoms," and ancestors alike. What's more, in this city at this time, real estate transactions never took place without a considerable part scripted for construction workers. It hardly seems surprising, then, that Nadar habitually included one of their number in his pictures as well. Obviously he couldn't ask a living man to pose for the necessary 18-minute exposure time (though he did make one self-portrait in the catacombs), so he made do with a mannequin that he brought along with him *(fig. 5.7)*. Flexible, versatile, and lifelike, this mannequin pushes wagons, shovels, and bones in numerous pictures, a strangely compelling symbol of the living among the once-alive in an era in which the boundaries between life and death had begun to blur. Given the emphasis on roadways, movement, and active work, Nadar's catacombs don't seem like a place where the words "Nothingness" or "Vain Grandeur, silence! Eternity!" should be inscribed on the walls.[53] They seem, indeed, like a pretty busy place: continually in process, designed for circulation, redistribution, and change.

The same, though to a much greater extent, is true of Nadar's sewers. These he saw as forming a vast network, a system geared toward "a permanent evolution"—though he did look for a sewer that could live up to its reputation for being "the black rendezvous of the immense Nothingness." [54] To Nadar, as to Victor Hugo, the sewers represented the Romantic "synthesis of all our Parisian life:" the ending of civilization, the place where history, individuality, and societal distinctions dissolved into the primal ooze. Hugo wrote in *Les Misérables:*

> *The history of men is reflected in the history of the cloacae. In old Paris, the sewer is the rendezvous of all depletions and all attempts. . . . The sewer is the conscience of the city. All things converge into it and are confronted with one another. In this lurid place there is darkness, but there are no secrets. Each thing has its real form, or at least its definitive form. . . . All the uncleanliness of civilization, once it is out of service, falls into this pit of truth, where the immense slippage is brought to an end. . . . Here, no more false appearances . . . absolute nakedness . . . nothing more but what is, wearing the sinister face of what is ending."* [55]

Yet Hugo, like Nadar, was only too well aware that this image of the romantic, mysterious sewer—like the Old Paris it had served—had slipped into the past, a casualty of history. Or rather, the image was still alive, but physical reality no longer corresponded to it; and clearly Hugo preferred the old days, when there was "mire, but soul." [56] For the nineteenth century had decided that waste, like corpses, must be subject to order and control in the City of the Industrial Age. The Parisian underground in the 1860s was the product of an administrative decision that the Age of Reason must shed its light into the depths; no longer repositories of fear, those depths acquired, during the Second Empire, "an official aspect." [57] The sewers Nadar found— "neat, cold, straight, correct" [58]—were the new sewers, the ones that Haussmann had built. The prefect and Eugène Belgrand, his head of Water and Sewer Services (and the man who gave Nadar permission to work underground) were, in 1861, in the midst of revamping, extending, and rebuilding the entire sewer network. By 1870 Paris had 348 miles of sewers, four times the total in 1851; a system of collectors had been built to carry all waste water to the Seine below Paris; and a new, more efficient series of egg-shaped galleries, constructed of hydraulic cement, carried not only water and waste but mechanical cleaning machines called "sluice cars." [59]

These are the sewers that were visible to Nadar's camera in 1861. His pictures of the channels, crossroads, arcades, and machinery are clean-lined, geometric, indeed among the most abstract works produced during the Second Empire. Just as there were (to his amazement and suspicion) no signs of rats or poisons here, there were also no hints of the mystery or foulness that had inspired such horror of the "stink hole." All smelly vestiges of the past—like the stones of the city and the bones of its dead—had been laundered by the new, efficient underground system, geared toward the perpetual "circulation of mud."

Nadar's points of view in his sewer photographs were chosen to express this constant movement. The images are most often constructed on the diagonal or in such a way that the sewer galleries plunge rapidly back into deep space, giving the photographs a dynamism most often associated during those years with pictures of the new, wide boulevards (by Charles Marville, for example) or the railroads (as photographed by Edouard-Denis Baldus). His image of the galleries under the Pont au Change, for instance *(fig. 5.⁸)*, depicts the architectural arcade, almost centered in the picture, as it recedes into darkness. But this balanced composition is set in motion by the abstract forms that surround it—and that forge numerous connections between this picture and the Constructivist works of the first quarter of the twentieth century. The open-ended egg-shaped gallery encircling the arcade swings the image toward the left, a movement reiterated by the horizontal tracks of the sluice cars. Since this is a crossroad, the tracks moving on the diagonal from right to left are intersected by others plunging back into deep space, their linear forms enlivened by the circles of the turntable between them and the stripes of a grill in the middle ground.

This dynamism is also evident in the photograph of a sluice car stationed in the Chambre du Pont Notre-Dame *(fig. 5.⁹)*, but here it is enhanced by

fig 5.⁸
Nadar, *The Sewers under the Pont au Change,* 1861
(Bibliothèque Nationale, Paris)

a drama of light and darkness. Nadar's lighting equipment, installed on a modi-
fied car, is completely visible in this image (and, it should be added, its mechanical forms seem completely at home in this environment). The picture moves on
the diagonal from lower left to middle right, and the light, too, is aimed in that
direction; its intense illumination at the center of the photograph serves to high-
light the architectural geometries and the funnellike form of the gallery, which
seems to pull both light and machinery into the recesses of darkness at the right.

As an image of pure motion, though, probably nothing in Nadar's oeuvre surpasses his picture of the crossroads of the sewage collectors *(fig. 5.*[10]*)*.
Emphasizing its function as a place of exchange, Nadar has photographed the

fig 5.[9]

Nadar, *The Sewers at the Chambre du Pont Notre-Dame,* 1861
(Bibliothèque Nationale, Paris)

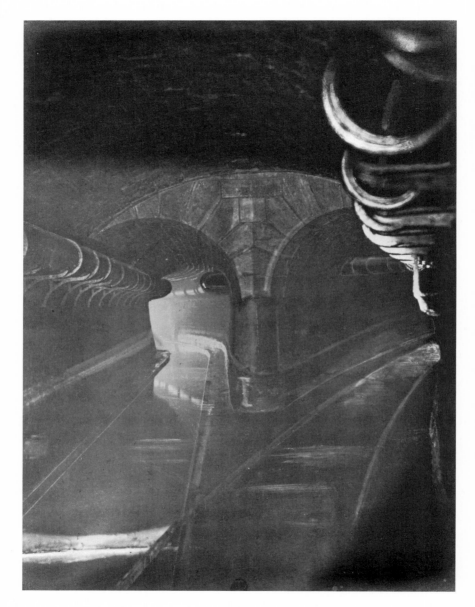

fig 5.[10]

Nadar, *Sewer Junction,* 1861 (Bibliothèque Nationale, Paris)

intersection in such a way that the viewer can see the two galleries meet in the foreground and then separate as they sweep backward, one toward the left and the other toward the right. Their plunge into the spatial depths is reinforced by the spiraling forms of the pipes that line the side walls and that lead the eye backward to the brilliant light at the end of the tunnel on the left. Large in the foreground and then radically foreshortened as they move toward the rear, these pipes catch the highlights in such a way that they seem to become dematerialized forms of motion. Maybe at one time the Parisian sewers were a stopping place, an ending, a final graveyard of the slime and debris of history. In 1861, however, the slime moved ceaselessly through this underground city—an unpeopled metropolis whose roads and lights, like those of the refurbished city above, had been carefully planned to facilitate the circulation of traffic. Indeed, these subterranean thoroughfares even sported, as Nadar's pictures often show, their own street signs corresponding to the ones above ground.

This correspondence was, of course, not lost on people living in Paris during the Second Empire. Hugo himself wrote that "Paris has another Paris under herself: a Paris of sewers, which has its streets, its crossroads, its squares, its blind alleys, its arteries and its circulation, which is slime, minus the human form."[60] But when Charles Kunstler speaks of the underground as the "Double of Paris," and describes it as the "City of Shadows," he is expressing in the twentieth century a romantic conception that, Nadar found, was not even appropriate by the second half of the nineteenth.[61] Far from being a shadowy counterpart of its sister city above, the Parisian underground was already, in Nadar's time, an exact reflection of that newly ordered municipality—right down to the specifics of its architecture, since the sewers comprised a space "where each discharging mouth is an arcade (and) the Rue de Rivoli sets the fashion even in the cloaca."[62] Nadar's photographs document a subterranean city whose shadows had been vanquished by gaslights; the shades of the past, of the dead, of the used up and discarded were being flooded with the light of reason—and the artificial light from Nadar's own equipment.

For Nadar's desire to map and make public mysterious realms heretofore uncharted by the camera was, in itself, a part of the zeitgeist of Haussmannization. The prefect himself had provided the city with its first accurate survey map; Nadar, journeying into the depths of the earth and the past, emerged with the first photographic records of the once invisible underbelly of Paris. Three years before that, he had succeeded in mapping the city from above: it was he who, using an aerial balloon, took the first bird's-eye view photographs of Paris.

Maps

In his book *Mémoires du Géant,* Nadar explained how his interest in aerial photography was a natural outgrowth of his interest in mapping. Specifically, he was seeking alternatives to the laborious and inaccurate processes of surveying necessary to transcribe a bird's-eye view.[63] His pioneering work once again involved a patent and much experimentation, since the obstacles to his efforts included not only the motion of the balloon's gondola but also escaping gas (which ruined the initial plates) and his equipment's overall weight (which he was able to offset only by removing some of his clothes before takeoff). Nadar built "Le Géant," *(fig. 5.¹¹)* a balloon six times normal size, as a publicity stunt to earn money for his real obsession, heavier-than-air flying machines. In his insistence that such machines would finally conquer the skies—as well as in his strategic use of the balloon during the Siege of Paris to deliver the first "air mail"—he was uncommonly foresighted. However, here as elsewhere, this artist's prophecies always looked backward as much as forward, drawing their inspiration, Januslike, from the past: in essence Nadar's attraction to flying was a Romantic one. His passion for the skies was based on a search for the sublime, for what he called the "infinite voluptuousness of silence." He elaborated this in impossibly purple prose in his essay in "Le Dessus et le dessous de Paris":

*There only complete detachment, real solitude. . . . (In) the limitless im-
mensity of these hospitable and benevolent spaces where no human force,
no power of evil can reach you, you feel yourself living for the first time,
because you enjoy as never before the plenitude of your health of soul and
body, and the proud feeling of your liberty invades you. . . . The healthy
altitude that now distances you reduces all things to the proportions of
truth. . . . In this supreme isolation, in this superhuman spasm, . . . the
body forgets itself; it exists no longer, and the detached soul is going to
surprise the mysterious word [sic] of eternal problems."*[65]

fig 5.[11]
Nadar, *Le Géant, 2nd ascension from the Champs de Mars*, October 18, 1863
(Bibliothèque Nationale, Paris)

Isolation, silence, the body forgotten, things reduced to the proportions of truth: in such terms did the Romantic imagination cast all places and experiences—from the sewers to the skies—that transcended normal reference points of time and space. The sublime connections between death and ballooning had been drawn by the architect Boullée as early as 1784 (on the heels of the Montgolfier brothers' flight) in his design for a cenotaph to Newton: a huge, empty spherical structure, illuminated to resemble alternatively the radiant sun and the night sky. In this vast "landscape" where normal spatial relations and markers were suspended, the architect wanted the viewer to experience the immensity of the cosmos described by the great physicist and astronomer: a cosmos "in which the onlooker finds himself as if by magic floating in the air, borne in the wake of images in the immensity of space."[65]

Nadar looked to the skies, as he looked to the sewers and catacombs, in his quest for a void where the spirit could be free—where, liberated from normal physical and societal laws, the "detached soul" could experience what he called "the Soul of the Earth." But it was only in the highest reaches of the clouds that he found the death that liberates, that allows one to "feel (oneself) living for the first time." When he looked, not up, but down at his native city, he found a death of another sort entirely.

That death, of course, is not visible in the pictures, of which there are few. The photographs show us Haussmann's Paris, as it stood in 1858. Nadar's balloon took off from the Champs de Mars, and he glimpsed therefore the northwest of Paris, the area most built up by the prefect to accommodate the residential movements of the rich bourgeoisie. The picture labeled the *First Result (fig. 5.12)* (which might not, in fact, have been published until much later in the century) shows the new roads, as well as buildings and landmarks like the Parc Monceau, the Russian Church, Montmartre in the distance, and the Arc de Triomphe, at the lower right and cut by the frame. The arch is the centerpiece of another picture *(fig. 5.13),* taken from closer down, as the Etoile on which it stood was the centerpiece of Haussmann's urban scheme and his favorite accomplishment. Lacking horizon lines and flattening deep space, an image like this

fig 5.[12]

Nadar, picture labeled "First Result" of aerial photography, 1858? or later
(Bibliothèque Nationale, Paris)

fig 5.[13]
Nadar, aerial photograph of Paris, 1858 (Bibliothèque Nationale, Paris)

one shows the geometric sweeps of the great avenues as they demarcate the land and unify monuments, buildings, and neighborhoods into one total spectacle of the urban environment.

Though these are the first aerial photographs, there are precedents for this type of imagery in bird's-eye maps and paintings, as well as in the panoramic photographs discussed earlier, which were widely disseminated at exactly the moment in the 1860s when the effects of Haussmann's new network of boulevards, many of them completed or in the process of completion by this time, were being strongly felt in the life of the city. In his aerial photograph of the Arc de Triomphe, Nadar has documented this process of transition. Only four wide streets are clearly visible here (ultimately twelve were built), and they radiate from the Etoile, serving as the "arteries in the urban circulatory system" that Paris was rapidly becoming.[66] It is by means of these roads, which themselves provide the order shaping the organism of the city, taking precedence in scale and importance over monuments, buildings, and neighborhoods, that one best understands Haussmannization. For the prefect's new city was about circulation: about traffic, efficient movement, and, as Nadar said about the sewers, "permanent evolution." In the clean sweep of their diagonals, in their geometrical organization, in their focus on crossroads and places of exchange, the photographs of Paris itself are indeed the doubles of the photographs of the underground. Though their subjects differ widely, the underlying structures of the photographs in all three series are very much related, because the new urban order was everywhere. All of Nadar's documentary images of Paris, whether taken above or below the ground, are about dynamism, circulation, change, and, as a result, about a new, thoroughly modern kind of death.

To Nadar in the 1850s and 1860s, change spelled the doom of the *this has been*. When he looked down from his balloon at his native city, he could not recognize what he saw; he was "like a traveler who arrived yesterday in a strange city." In this new Paris, one couldn't "take two steps without falling in the quagmire of some new embellishment, conceived in its maturity from the eve to the night, decreed in the morning, and executed a quarter of an hour before." This, in his mind, was a "transformed, confused Paris . . . (where) all is changed, up-set, ideas, things, even names." His photographs might be static, frozen, stopped in the flow of time. But they describe a place where "all that is provisional is eternal, except the governments. . . . Of marble here, there is nothing, and I am among those who will have nothing to claim at the hour when the definitive bill is presented: the True."

The True. In his Paris pictures as in his portraits, Nadar was searching for the eternal in the ephemeral—and he found, whether in the catacombs, the sewers, or the city itself, only the transitory, whose definitive price was the sacri-fice of the True. "I hope," he wrote in "Le Dessus et dessous de Paris" at the start of his journey into the air, "that we will finish by finding the heart of this place." What he found instead was that there was no heart, no eternal truth left, that it too had been demolished and rebuilt in this metropolis where the only constant was change. This new, shiny, bustling city was a *this is* without a *this has been*, and so, for Nadar, it existed no longer: "It is no longer Paris, my Paris that I know, where I was born. . . . I no longer know how to find myself in that which surrounds me."

Nadar's pilgrimages into the underground and the sky must, ultimately, be seen as searches for himself: for the memories, dreams, mysteries, and images that he attached to the place of his birth. He brought with him the most modern technologies; he documented and mapped in the most accurate, detailed way possible; he was able to stop, in his prints, the flow of time and change. But even the most advanced image-making techniques couldn't retrieve the subjectivity, the soul, the truth of a place where "they have destroyed everything, down to the last *souvenir* . . . (where) something of us has gone away." The Paris that Nadar and his camera see is one in which there are no people—and not only because they are too far away, too small to see from a balloon, or too quick for exposure times underground. Rather, Nadar's is a Paris from which all traces of people have "gone away," leaving a city full of physical objects, even "exterior charm," but empty, dead, devoid of spirit. Nadar, like Louis Blanc, saw in the transformation of Paris the end of memory; the end of the unaffected merger of the physical and the spiritual, of the past and the present; the end, that is, of life.

In looking at Haussmann's Paris, the artist might as well have been contemplating the catacombs, where dispersed skulls and sternum bones consigned to oblivion all history and subjectivity. For he whose life had begun and unfolded in this place could find no trace of *himself* in this strange city: of his past, of his emotional bonds, of the memories that formed the unchanging image of Paris in his mind.

As the sewers attempted to launder the city's filth, so this new Paris tried to wash away those memory traces of the self that personalize urban space. Nadar nonetheless knew, sadly, that the "illustrious phantoms" never disappear. As he surveyed the official, clean, orderly sewers, he cautioned his readers to remember that "poison is no less poison for being latent." He felt the same way as he viewed his native city from a balloon. Haussmann might have succeeded in changing the face of Paris, but he could only dispossess, and never destroy, the past. Nadar knew that the shadows of Paris persisted too, latent in the handsome boulevards, splendid cafés, and grand monuments, and to him they were the poison that was destined to kill all life and love in this City of the Industrial Age.

For these shadows were now forced to dwell exclusively in the minds of Paris's inhabitants, alienating them irreparably from any unmitigated experience of the metropolis. Baudelaire best described this disjunction between the external world and his internal perception of it in his poem "The Swan":

> *Paris changes . . . but in sadness like mine*
> *nothing stirs — new buildings, old*
> *neighborhoods turn to allegory*
> *and memories weigh more than stone.*[67]

Both Baudelaire and Nadar were living in a time warp: a historical moment when "memories weigh(ed) more than stone" while the stones of the city crumbled like paper; when mental images remained immobile, while the world did not. Experience itself, in this context, became like a photograph: "motionless, (it) flow(ed) back(ward)," while the city around it swam on in time, caught up in a "permanent evolution" of progress and change.

This is, of course, the same evolution documented in Nadar's Paris pictures, static images caught up in the dynamism of Haussmann's world. Here lies the final paradox of Nadar's photographs of Paris: motionless though they are, they refuse to flow backward. In this they are the diametric opposites of the famous portraits. Both series, in different ways, involved Nadar's search for the self. In the portraits, that self was a living presence; it revealed its eternity in its ephemera, it spoke its spirit in physical form. For that reason, these pictures are very much about the preservation of life, and thus of memory. In the Paris pictures, on the other hand, Nadar chose to document the sites from which the self had been evicted, where there was nothing left to preserve. No matter how much light he shed, no matter how detailed a map he made, the pictures could, finally, only be records of absence, of death: of a *this is* severed from its *this has been,* and thus severed from its roots in time. His static photographs could document the changing, dynamic city, but they were powerless to retrieve those memory images that gave Paris its eternal meaning and that now found their final resting place in the artist's heart. For a camera could not remember, it could only record; it could not feel, it could only see. It could never, therefore, express the truth that existed in the chasm between Nadar's eye and his mind.

So his pictures do not attempt to preserve the past, or express his nostalgia, or serve as memory substitutes. They function, rather, as Barthesian "countermemories": images that "block memory . . . (because they) fill the sight by force, and because in them nothing can be refused or transformed." [68] They, like the metropolis they depict, fill the eye with spectacles that exist without past and without future: *this is* for all eternity. To Nadar and his friends, there was no transformation possible in Haussmann's Paris, for in spite of all the hustle and bustle this city could no longer move in time—a movement that must go backward to go forward. And there could be no substitute for memory. Photography could record the physical appearance of the city, but it could no more build a bridge between the past and the present than it could resurrect the body of Victor Hugo. This comparison, it seems, is particularly apt. Perhaps the Paris pictures are, in fact, Nadar's most ironic contribution to deathbed photography.

VI

Voyages without Steam or Sail:
Afterimages from the Floating Head

B audelaire never wrote about trains. The world in which he lived was one of colors, of scents, of correspondences—natural and cultural—of an unbearable intensity, a world in which the memories of other lives and spaces bled into each other at will. He lived in the Paris of the nineteenth century, but in reality he never walked those streets; only once in his Parisian poems does he mention a specific place, the new Place du Carrousel in "The Swan," and he does so only to move the scene into its afterimage, into its counterpart in memory.[1] As discussed in chapter 1, this man wandered through the city "stumbling over words like cobblestones,"[2] his real experience of the physical world constantly mediated by the allegoric, continually transmuted into words that could express a vision only tangentially connected to the people and places that formed the network of his existence.

This world of shifting times and spaces, of dreams that bleed willy-nilly into the physical and often dispossess it completely, was, however, the world embodied by the advent of trains.

Archetypes of technological power, these machines nevertheless helped to create the reality of evanescence that greatly transformed the perceptions of those living in the nineteenth century. At once we enter the culture of mediated experience; the culture of movement and change; the culture of afterimages and visions that fly by, leaving our subjectivity floating in a space that is, in truth, a nonspace. The landscape traversed by the trains is a landscape transformed by technology into a panorama, a passage in which life becomes art—and art itself turns into an allegory of the real.

If one is, truly, to understand the modernism that came into being in France during the 1850s, one must, a priori, perceive these transitions, these movements toward a subjectivity no longer inexorably linked to the physical world. "These travels by steam keep on shaking the world—in which there really is nothing left but railway stations—like a kaleidoscope," wrote Joseph von Eichendorff.[3] Passing through the landscape like projectiles, cutting through towns and villages, flying through a nature that seems, in comparison, small and quaint, these "flying salons" telescoped time and space much as did the new craze for travel photography, which came of age at the same moment as the trains, twin cornerstones in the vision that was to be modernity.

Simultaneously, as if movement and stasis were one and the same, the culture provided a means to see the planet and to bring the world to those who preferred their own salons. One remained at home, yet even then time and space refused to remain still. With the availability of photographic images, especially the popular stereographs, distances were bridged in the form of circulating pictures: a new, allegorical form of traffic. Notre-Dame and the Parthenon, Turkish steles and the Taj Mahal, the Holy Lands and the Alps *(figs. 6.¹, 6.², 6.³)* came to visit, in two dimensions instead of three, disembodied from their time and space—their Benjaminian "aura."[4] This kaleidoscopic vision, mediated by technology, turned the entire planet into one luminous network in space—seen always through either the lens of a camera or the window of a train.

Let us not forget the similarities between these two "windows" onto the world: the rectangles through which we of the modern world perceive what we think of as physical reality. On a very basic level, both trains and cameras are machines that channel the vision of the spectator. Their common origins are evident when Jonathan Crary, in *Techniques of the Observer,* points out the importance of the Diorama of Louis J. M. Daguerre, later to become the inventor of photography. Unlike the static panorama paintings invented by Barker in the 1780s, the Diorama was a "machine of wheels in motion"[5] consisting of a room with two apertures through which the audience perceived different painted scenes and changing light effects—when the circular platform on which the observers stood changed position. The autonomy of the spectator was lost; one

fig 6.[1]

Jean Walther, *The Parthenon,* from Blanquart-Evrard (editor),
Artiste et Amateur, 1851 (Bibliothèque Nationale, Paris)

fig 6.[2]

Louis de Clerq, *Seventh Station of the Cross, (where Jesus fell for the second time),* 1859 (Bibliothèque Nationale, Paris)

fig 6.[3]
Bisson Brothers (L. A. and A. R.), *Savoie*, 1860
(Bibliothèque Nationale, Paris)

saw through the mediator of the machine. Point of view became, not an ideal position, but one that incorporated the temporality of the situation, involuntary movements dictated by the rhythms of technology.

So it is, of course, with trains—those windows onto the world in which one's body is, to quote Ruskin, "a living parcel."[6] Mobility of vision has become normalized perception—as Wolfgang Schivelbusch explains, since the traveler can "only see things in motion . . . this vision no longer experience(s) evanescence: evanescent reality ha(s) become the new reality."[7] Merged into a machine cutting through the landscape, unable to relate with sensory intensity to the environs, the observer speeds by a panorama whose component parts lose their tactility and become instead successive visions bleeding into afterimages, phantasmagoria heightening the unreality of the nonspace within which one sits. Small wonder Eichendorff noted that the world had become nothing but railway stations; they were the only objects that stood still—besides, of course, photographs. Like these light pictures, stations were still points marking the geographic delineations of a finite landscape whose boundaries were defined by the visitations of technology.

Travelers in the nineteenth century, not yet habituated to the phenomena of speed, noticed the changes in perception, the shifts in intensities, that characterized passage on the train. Instead of changes in geography, instead of cultural differences and local color, the voyager locked in a compartment saw the passing views simply as a series of disembodied images. "He (the traveler) hardly knows the names of the principal cities through which he passes, and only recognizes them, if at all, by the steeples of the best-known cathedrals that appear like trees by some faraway road,[8] wrote a French medical author in 1857. The landscape itself — once carved and straightened, leveled and cut by the tracks that needed not nature's but culture's artificial geometries to function—was transformed by the speed of its passage into a montage of successive vistas whose particularities became harder to grasp. "Dreamlike traveling on the railroad," wrote Emerson in 1843.[9] "The towns which I pass . . . make no distinct impression. They are like pictures on a wall." The world as photograph, visual representation that has lost its connection to the body and its roots in time and space.

Small wonder that photography and trains came of age in France at the same moment. The windows onto the world that are photographs—the images already cut, already mediated by technology—are static; they are, perhaps, the apotheosis of the point of view of the spectator, frozen for perusal. But then again, as this point of view was packaged and transformed into one element of the image traffic that flourished during this period, individual vision too became a "parcel," functioning in an extra-personal network farther reaching even than the tentacular tracks of the train. It is important to remember, in this context, that travel photography in the nineteenth century—a major focus of the medium from the beginning of its history—was always conceived of in relation to art reproduction. The same century that gave us the idea of a public museum, in which booty from various cultures could be trapped and displayed, also invented the notion of "taking" photographic impressions of a culture in order to gain knowledge, and therefore at least intellectual control, over its patrimony. Records of a body in motion whose perceptions too can travel the world, uprooted vision that roams the cultures of the earth in order to deliver parcels of sensibility to your home, photographs codified the global village, fleshing out the map of the imagination that geographical space had become, transmuting space into two-dimensional images that became the railway stations of the mind.

I

Physical space is, of course, more than physical: it is, ultimately, a mental space, that map of the imagination that defines for us the parameters within which we move. The nineteenth century redrew this map by artificially extending our sense perceptions in myriad ways, of which photography and trains are only two. On the one hand, the railroads, by making it possible to travel from one locale to another in greatly diminished time, brought cities and towns infinitely closer to each other; but on the other hand, as distances were bridged, so were mental concepts of geography and culture, local identities that had always been determined by the spaces between places. "What changes must now occur, in our way of looking at things, in our notions!," wrote Heinrich Heine. "I feel as if the mountains and forests of all countries were advancing on Paris. Even now, I can smell the German linden trees; the North Sea's breakers are rolling against my door." [10] Space became, in a way, elastic, malleable like a rubber band, as the primacy of national and geographic differences was destroyed by speed; unleashed from their moorings, destinations refused to stay in their place.

The map of the imagination began to resemble the Surrealists' *rencontre* of the umbrella and the sewing machine on a dissecting table: luminous, disjointed, and yet linked by an almost uncanny simultaneity. "Space is killed by the railways," Heine continued, "and we are left with time alone." [11] Paris to Lyon becomes, in this equation, two hours: a temporal equivalent to what used to be a physical experience. Since the passenger thinks only of his or her destination while trapped in the nonspace of the speeding projectile, the traversed landscape, barely noticed, becomes a mental construct whose boundaries are defined by clocks and watches—a perceptual switch that eventually gave rise to the imposition of global standard time in 1912. Baudelaire's dictum, that the ultimate modernist experience was to be a kaleidoscope gifted with consciousness, [12] describes the travels of the floating head through charted space illuminated not only by train stations but by timepieces whose tyranny, by the twentieth century, encircled the globe.

Baudelaire's poem "Travelers" from *Les Fleurs du Mal* is relevant here, to give us a vision of the consciousness coming of age in the era of steam travel. [13] Dedicated to Maxime Du Camp, the writer and photographer of the Middle East mentioned earlier, the poem is this book's longest, and describes a world whose parameters are fluid, flexible, and ultimately a faculty of mind. "The child enthralled by lithographs and maps / can satisfy his hunger for the world: / how limitless it is beneath the lamp / and how it shrinks in the eyes of memory!" The nineteenth century opened up unparalleled vistas to the human traveler: for the first time, mass transit was accessible to many, exotic landscapes came into view (whether by train or photograph); the fruits of all of human civilization became available to the sight, an enormous marketplace within which one chose one's victuals. This metaphoric connection between commodity culture and travel is not, of course, fortuitous: the 1850s gave us both the first department stores and the trains that supplied them with their constantly changing supply of goods, those literal parcels that accompanied their human counterparts on their voyages. And what links these two examples of nineteenth-century ingenuity is, as Baudelaire writes, *desire.*

The world that Baudelaire describes in "Travelers"—a world in which people are constantly moving, constantly fleeing, searching for novelties whether through voyages or the lust for images of the exotic—is ultimately not so different from that described by Zola in his novel about department stores, *Au Bonheur des Dames.*[14] It is a world where boredom and spiritual ennui are alleviated by attempts to act out our dreams: "We long to journey without steam or sail!/ Help us forget the prison of our days." In the context of early capitalism, commodity fetishes, like dreams about far away cultures, were the keys that promised to unlock the prison of the present: the "plunge" into the "abyss . . . to find the *new*" (his emphasis). It is, it seems, no coincidence that this poem was the final statement in *Les Fleurs du Mal,* in the edition published during his lifetime. For it describes a world whose inhabitants are condemned—damned, we should say—to a constant spiral of desire, whose arena became, more and more, the entire surface of the globe.

Yet this spiral already, by Baudelaire's time, was closed; it was, as he knew well, a trap. Like Marcel Duchamp's shop window, that display case that must not be broken or trespassed lest fulfillment end in disappointment, Baudelaire's world of travel was, ultimately, solipsistic, a planet whose surface could only retain its sparkle if never traversed. "Our soul is a schooner seeking a free port,/ and when the question rises from the deck,/ a voice from the topmast eagerly replies/ 'Happiness! . . . Glory! . . . Love! . . .' Another reef." What the traveler—he whose search for exoticism and novelty pulled him, like a balloon in the wind, through long awaited vistas—found was that life was the same everywhere, that cultural differences were only the embellishments masking the sameness of the human condition, "the boring pageant of immortal sin": "It is a bitter truth our travels teach!/Tiny and monotonous, the world/has shown— will always show us—what we are:/oases of fear in the wasteland of ennui!" Limitless beneath the lamp, the world as it appears to the eyes—and to the eyes of memory, frozen on a photographic plate—is a hunger that can never be appeased, a finite system doomed to closure by the railroad ties that leveled the land and shattered the shop window of the spirit.

II

This discussion of closure and of finite space brings us, of course, to maps, those linchpins of nineteenth-century technological modernism. Building rails and cities depends, of course, on mapping: on accurate surveys that describe, mark, name, and in so doing delineate the parameters of a terrain, and the nineteenth century gave us men like Haussmann and Nadar who learned to exploit the power contained in these miniaturized representations. Mapping is, of course, a process that greatly extends intellectual control while simultaneously abstracting conceptual knowledge from lived experience. Completely mediated, one's understanding of space from a map confounds, indeed contradicts, the experience of the body in time and place.

Those writing during the mid-1850s, caught in full awareness by the immediacy of these newly created perceptual patterns, attempted to describe the ever-widening gaps between one's *lived* and *imagined* experience of space. Constantin Pecqueur, writing in 1839, described it in this way: "By a sort of miracle every man's field would be found not only where it always was, but as large as ever it was. Every bit of terrain, each field on this surface would still remain intact; so would every house in a village, the village itself, or the town;

every territory with its village in the center would remain a province; on the map of the imagination, all of these would finally be reproduced and reduced down to the infinitely small! As for Louvres, or Pontoise, or Chartres, or Arpajon, etc., it is obvious that they will just get lost in some street of Paris or its suburbs." [15] Seemingly "limitless beneath the lamp," the world once charted was reduced to the infinitely small—the map of the imagination, easily reproduced and controlled, set out the parameters by which the shrinking of the planet could occur.

Baudelaire, in "Travelers," focused of course on the sameness of the human condition, the uniformity that in essence made all voyages redundant. His was a spiritual quest, but maps in a sense are the intellectual counterparts of his psychic discoveries. Standard time was imposed by law, but standard space was imposed by maps: abstract and uniform languages that could, indeed, be used to describe any terrain and any culture, no matter where. The map of the imagination was charted in advance, fixed and frozen like a photographic image, systematized, homogenized, linked to symbols that refused the sensory intensities of geographical and national differences. "Henceforth," Baudrillard has written, "it (was) the map that preceded the territory . . . It (was) the map that engendered the territory." [16] Anchors for human beings set in motion, the maps themselves began to define the limitations imposed on minds, and bodies, supposedly set free.

Erwin Straus, in contrasting the difference between a landscape and the geographical space that became the norm in the nineteenth century, greatly enhances our capacity to see the perceptual shifts that determined spatial experience in the era of the trains. "In a landscape," he wrote, "we always get to one place from another place; each location is determined only by its relation to the neighboring place within the circle of visibility. But geographical space is closed, and is therefore in its entire structure transparent. Every place in such a space is determined by its position with respect to the whole and ultimately by its relation to the null point of the coordinate system by which this space obtains its order. Geographical space is systemized." [17] The space on a map is closed, defined; it has already, in essence, been explored; the map itself exists in a way as the memory, the afterimage of the original voyage. The landscape becomes transparent because it has already been traversed. The voyage of the body, seen from this perspective, becomes a déjà vu.

Or a million déjà vus, a million perspectives on an experience that has already been defined. The nineteenth century in its splendor was the century of technological wonders, of trains whose awesome power became the symbol of human progress. One's floating subjectivity, as one traveled with increasing speed on the trains, became a mystical experience, a merger with this power, a transformation of point of view into the generalized consciousness of the age. It is as if these maps, these guides to this new territory of the spirit, were icons charting the stations of the railway as earlier ages had visualized the Stations of the Cross.

It is in this context that one must see the "Carte Illustré of the Northern Railroad Lines: Itinerary from Paris to Boulogne" *(fig. 6.4)*, long attributed to Edouard Baldus. Done on commission for the banker James de Rothschild, this work is an achievement that links two of the great technological wonders of the age: trains and photographs. This illustrated map is linked to a project originally conceived in 1855, when Queen Victoria came to France—the first official visit by an English sovereign since 1431—and celebrated the opening of the Paris-Boulogne line. Created in just three days (mostly from photographs already in Baldus's inventory) as a gift for the queen, the original album was conceived, in effect, as a souvenir in advance, an anticipation not only of her journey on the new railroad but also of her need to retain her memories in permanent form.

Consisting of fifty large-format photographs depicting views of towns, monuments, and sites along the line (for instance, *figs. 6.5, 6.6*), arranged essentially in the order in which these vistas would have been perceived by the queen (had she, of course, not been speeding past them like a bullet), the original work functions within the tradition not only of travel books and photographic albums of the time but also of sumptuous picture surveys like the *Excursions Daguerriennes,* published in 1841 and 1843 and consisting of drawings based on photographic images. According to Malcolm Daniels, who has done a serious study

of the train albums,[18] this sumptuous art work was enough of a success to suggest to Rothschild that he commission—somewhat later—twenty-five supple-
mentary copies to give to the administrative council of the Northern Railroad.
The illustrated map is the second volume of this later, "mass-produced" work,
and Daniels has convincingly suggested that this map was actually composed for
the most part of images by Furne fils and H. Tournier (specialists in stereographic photographs) and other less illustrious amateurs in about 1860. For the
sake of ease, this essay will continue to refer to the work as Baldus's conception,
but Daniels's point is well argued and well taken.

I will, however, take exception to his conclusion that the hackneyed
quality of many of the images and the multiple authors involved in the project
disqualify this as a "product worthy to be dignified within the firmament of the
fine arts." [19] Such a judgment completely obliterates the originality of nineteenth-
century photographic experimentation in general and of this work in particular.
This "Carte Illustré," an enormous map surrounded with and covered by photographs, is probably the closest thing we have to a visualization of the "luminous
explosion in space" that were the railroads. Designed and executed not as an art
work but on assignment, it nevertheless, at least conceptually if not aesthetically,
stands at the cutting edge of nineteenth-century photographic modernism.

Less an illustration of a voyage than a symbolic recreation, the "Carte
Illustré" consists of six panels linked together and folded in a leather album. On
these panels are pasted a map, with the trajectory of the railroad line highlighted,
and seventy-two photographic images. Unfurled, the entire work measures 418
by 1444 cm. Unwieldy in its serpentine shape that exceeds arms' reach and thus
begins to undermine the intimate scale of most photographic works, the piece
gives the impression of extending outward in ways that stretch both the physical
body and the eyes' capacity to view an image all at once. It is, in fact, impossible
to take in at a glance the whole sweep of the six panels, the whole overview
of this journey, so the work itself becomes by definition a panorama. Yet this
breadth is at once in conflict with the scale of the photos: tiny, miniaturized in
fact, these views scattered around the borders and pasted onto the map itself

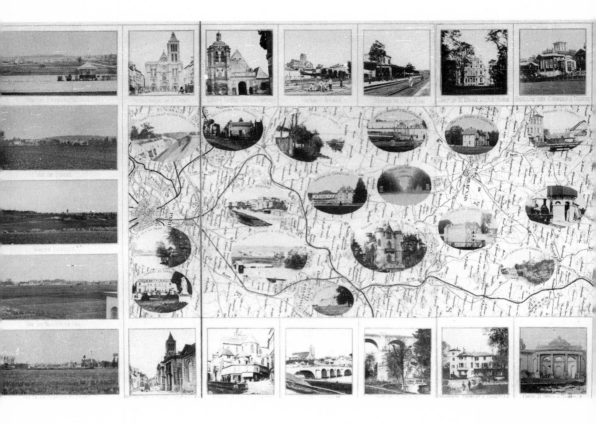

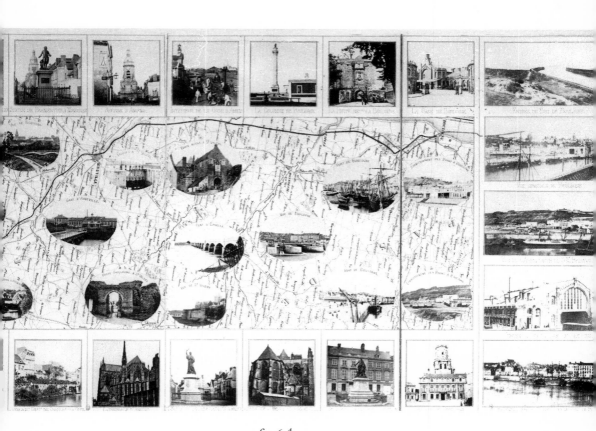

fig 6.[4]
Attributed to E. Baldus (more probably by Furne fils and H. Tournier), *Chemin de Fer du Nord, Ligne de Paris à Boulogne, Carte Illustré, Tome 2,* 1860 (Bibliothèque Nationale, Paris)

fig 6.[5]

E. Baldus, *View of Amiens,* from *Chemin de Fer du Nord, Tome 1,* 1855
(Bibliothèque Nationale, Paris)

fig 6.[6]

E. Baldus, *Amiens Station,* from *Chemin de Fer du Nord, Tome 1,* 1855
(Bibliothèque Nationale, Paris)

seem to embody Pecqueur's statement that Pointoise can "get lost in some street of Paris or its suburbs."

Seen in its multidimensionality, this work is a visualization of spatial time—or, on the other hand, temporal space. On the most basic level we are faced with a map delineating the territory from Paris to Boulogne. Lodged in that nexus point where physical experience has become representational and therefore conceptual, the map holds within it the complexity of the century's experience. But it also represents, in this context, not only the physical ground of Baldus's piece but its experiential ground as well: it chronicles, from left to right, the passage from one city to another, in the order within which these geographical locations would be experienced in time by the traveler. The drawn line represents a voyage, marked first by planners, then by machinery; transformed by technology into geographical space; and then experienced simultaneously by all passengers on a train and also in its duration by the successive waves of travelers who, from that moment in the 1850s until now, have followed this path. The map, in this sense, embodies ritual experience, but described, explained, and traced—from left to right, for its symbolic form links us not with a North-South axis but with Western *écriture*—in terms that make sense within human chronological experience.

Yet the abstract nature of experience represented by the map itself, shifting as it does between lived and conceptual realities—the past, present, and future—is exploded into other dimensions by the inclusion of the photographs. On the most mundane levels, of course, the photographs simply represent views of the landscapes, stations, villages, and towns on the route: any modern viewer would have no trouble understanding the trajectory traced by the liaison of these two media. But that comprehension in itself is telling that this work describes a vision of the world that was the archetype for a landscape coming into being.

This is, of course, a panoramic landscape: visualized not in hierarchies, with fixed points that focus our attention, it is instead a sweep, a symbolic representation of a world seen in its generalized structures and not its particularities. Moving horizontally, this is a nonhierarchical space whose transparency is as regularized as the railroad ties that level mountains and valleys. The world Baldus traces is one where connecting links take precedence over places, where indeed specific locations and objects—cities, monuments, bridges—are transformed into little more than railroad stations, destination points marking the movement and change that are the raison d'être of the travel experience. All of these views are equal here: points on a map, or pictures on a wall.

But these pictures are arranged on this wall in ways that constantly alter the perspectives of the spectator. Representing memory, of course, as well as marking places of importance on the trajectory, the twenty-four images around the border of the map are the largest in scale here. This particular format—a map with pictures around it, visualizing places of importance in the geographical space described—was not new: an example of a map produced in and of Paris in 1789 *(fig. 6.⁷)* anchors Baldus firmly within a pictorial tradition. What is new here, however, are the shifting perspectives of this work, as if the format itself were exploding into dimensions of time that alone can describe the experience of the rails.

The first thing to notice is that the pictures bordering the map—unlike the pictures on the map—respect no geographical order: mixed up into that uncanny simultaneity of the Surrealists, these towns and monuments become the umbrella and the sewing machine whose meeting place is no longer a table but a trajectory in space. Though photographs of Boulogne, the final destination of the line, border the right-hand side, Pontoise precedes St. Denis and Boulogne rubs shoulders with Abbeville and Amiens along the top and bottom of the map. Most curious, however, are the five views bordering the left-hand side of the work (two of them visible in *fig. 6.⁸)*. Panoramic images representing towns like Louvres and Villers-le-Bel, the photographs juxtapose these places in order, it seems, to transmute them into nonplaces. This is done structurally: all five pictures, in spite of their subjects, are in essence the same: wide in their viewpoint, insistent in their horizontality, and basically empty, they level geographical differences as efficiently as the technology of the railroad companies had before them. The only thing that distinguishes one locale from another is detail—a tree

VUE DE LOUVRES

VUE DE VILLERS LE BEL

fig 6.⁷
Anonymous, map of Paris, 1789 (Bibliothèque Nationale, Paris)
(preceding page)

fig 6.⁸
Attributed to Baldus (more probably by Furne fils and H. Tournier), detail of the
left border of the *Carte Illustré, Chemin de Fer Du Nord, Tome 2,* 1860
(Bibliothèque Nationale, Paris)

here, a far-off structure there—so that the images simultaneously represent and completely deny the specificity of the places they supposedly describe. They are the view from the train window, framing the horizontal passage of a uniform terrain as it speeds by.

Yet immediately, as one looks toward the photographs bordering the top and bottom (all of them rectangular) or those pasted onto the map (oval in format), physical reality reasserts itself—or at least symbolic representations thereof. Spatially, the effect of this juxtaposition of map and photo is fascinating, and here Baldus's use of the circular format is quite effective. One has the impression, looking at this work, that one is peering through the flat space of the map into cut-out windows on the world. The camera functions almost like a set of binoculars that bring into focus what was visible through a series of keyholes. Most of the pictures depict sites—views of towns and landscapes, châteaux and railroad stations—that are seen roughly chronologically, moving left to right, on the map itself. All miniaturized and juxtaposed, churches and stations, viaducts and tracks, form a melting pot here, a celebration of simultaneity with no hierarchical distinctions. A cathedral or a city hall, seen in this context, is part of the continuum, the traversed space, filled also by bridges and boats. Baldus's panorama is wide, his trajectory is simply filled by things, *n'importe quoi*, but this is also a passage whose viewpoint shifts perceptibly en route. Within the given narrative structure of the journey, the photographer continually alters his point of view. There are close-up depictions of monuments, and wide-angle landscapes; overviews of towns, and details of bridges and statues. This change of focus, and change of format, makes the keyhole vision very complex. There are continual changes in spatial orientation: between diagonals moving in deep space, straight-on photographs of objects that block deep space, and perspectival views whose depth seems infinite.

This spatial complexity is echoed in the shifts in iconography and point of view. Nature, culture, and technology move in and out of focus: not only does Baldus continually alter the viewpoint back and forth between the trajectory itself (the leveled landscape panoramas, the train tracks marking the terrain) and the sites and objects it links together, but he also constantly changes perspectives between the views "of the train" and "from the train" on the map. Binocular visions of the Pavillon de Courses at Chantilly and the Statue of Pierre L'Ermite at Amiens, typical tourist sights, are, in other words, juxtaposed freely with pictures, like the one depicting the Gare de Chantilly, that blithely depict the equipment that brings the traveler there.

This is significant: he makes no fixed choice between these two viewpoints, which are radically different, and that in itself sets up a tension that moves this piece into the ambiguous space of the nineteenth century. Earlier works, like some already discussed by Marville and Le Secq, defined "sites" from the point of view of the promeneur, or the individual monad; the viewpoint was clear, the monument itself was centered, often seen outside of its larger context and therefore essentially highlighted as an object, a touristic phenomena or a trace of culture. But Baldus makes continual movements between subjectivities: between the traditional perspective of the passenger in situ, the mediated viewpoint from the window, and the overt celebration of the technology, train or track, that provides this experience. A deeply modernist work, echoing the spatial schizophrenias of some of Degas's best paintings, this map unleashes the experience of travel from its moorings, simultaneously visualizing the shifting perspectives of the floating head.

As these perspectives shift, so of course do the time zones they represent. As the map symbolizes conceptual experience, abstracted from the physical world, the photographs represent—or seem to—the concretions of things in space, full of detail and static in a way one would never be able to see them from the train itself. The photographs slow the train to a stop: frozen, luminous, and absolutely immobile, they function as dead weights in the rushing corridors of hyperspace.

They are, in other words, like still images placed in the midst of a film, shifting the movement of the map from durational time to stop-time. Brakes in the railway journey, they promise an experience of monuments and places that is, in reality, impossible if one passes through the terrain on a train like a speeding bullet. "In a few hours, (the railway) shows you all of France, and before your eyes it unrolls its infinite panorama, a vast succession of charming tableaux, of novel surprises," wrote Jules Claretie, a Parisian journalist. "Of a landscape it shows you only the great outlines, being an artist versed in the ways of the masters. Don't ask it for details, but for the living whole." [20] Yet the photographs pasted onto Baldus's map belie this statement; their function is to give us those details that would, in an earlier century, have made this a landscape instead of geographical space.

In their stillness and their contemplativeness, these "pictures on a wall" symbolically recreate—two-dimensionally and uniquely visually—a world of concrete experience that train travel itself has denied. "The intensive experience of the sensuous world, terminated by the industrial revolution, underwent a resurrection in the new institution of photography," wrote Wolfgang Schivelbusch. [21] In the context of the rapid realities of the nineteenth century, these pictorial anchors, these frozen visions of objects and places, full of detail, are nostalgic reminders of a world that the continuum of the map and the tracks has made obsolete. The seventy-two photographs placed around Baldus's map like "luminous explosions in space" are literally afterimages—as well as fantasies that stimulate a desire of the five senses that will, in fact, never be satiated during the journey.

In this sense the photographic frames are as tantalizing and as elusive a visual stimulus as a shop window, or the window of the train. Embodiments of Baudelaire's unquenchable desire, these images—whether perused at home, seen as memories or as anticipations of future voyages—exist in the gap between conceptual and lived experience that so perplexed inhabitants of nineteenth-century France. Trapped between the "living whole" and the intensity of the details, the macrocosm and the microcosm, Baldus's map gives us both. Unsettled and unstable, this work is a stopgap between two experiences of time and space, and its complexity allows us to glimpse the problems faced by those image makers trying to describe a map-of-the-imagination-in-progress.

III

This task—the description of the spatial aspects of modern life—was, it seems, an issue discussed in photographic circles during the 1850s, and not simply on the level of aesthetics. Photographers were deeply aware of the more exciting challenges of their role in documenting a changing world, as is evident in critical commentary in magazines like *La Lumière*. During the same years when Baudelaire was formulating the critical opinions expressed about Constantin Guys in *The Painter of Modern Life*,[22] photographic writers like Ernest Lacan and Paul Nibelle were debating, if less colorfully, the responsibilities of the photographer. As early as 1852, long before impressionism hit the scene, these two writers were arguing that public life, "space and the crowd" were the crucial aspects of modern, urban existence that photographers were bound to explore.[23]

Baldus's map partakes of this space; it exemplifies what Georg Simmel has called the "intensification of nervous stimulation" that characterizes urban perception, "the swift and uninterrupted change of outer and inner stimuli."[24] As discussed in chapter 4, these perceptual patterns came to the foreground of popular consciousness before they surfaced in real life; as Wolfgang Schivelbusch has written, "what the opening of major railroads provided in reality—the easy accessibility of distant places—was attempted in illusion, in the decades immediately preceding that opening, by the 'panoramic' and dioramic shows and gadgets."[25]

The language used during this period to describe train travel, as noted in Jules Claretie's statement already quoted, that the evanescent landscape seen from the train window "unrolls its infinite panorama . . . before your eyes," makes it clear that voyagers were conscious of this connection: that they were aware that the fleeting vision passing before their eyes transformed life itself into art. This perception is not as curious as it seems, given the fact that the construction of the rails themselves involved the massive transformation of nature, the cutting, leveling, and building that were the pride of progress in the nineteenth century—a pride in technological beauty that is evident in the many photographs, by Baldus and especially Collard *(figs. 6.⁹, 6.¹⁰, 6.¹¹)*, of viaducts, tunnels, and bridges. This artful shaping of the land, this transmutation of nature into culture, organic into geometric, gave the early travelers almost the impression that the railroad itself was a theater: one purchased a ticket to a large-scale diorama whose views had been shaped for one's perusal. In this context, the voyage itself became the stage show and the passing world the spectacle, the technologically choreographed play.

This perception, so steeped in the Western notion that culture would, by definition, improve upon those raw and unfinished delights provided by nature, is evident in early writings about train travel, in appreciative comments about the roles the rails played in improving upon the aesthetics of the landscape. By 1830, for instance, Francis Lieber would write about a trip from Manchester to Liverpool in terms that underscore his admiration for the train's creation of pleasing perspectives on what might have once been a boring landscape:

The passenger by this new line of route having to traverse the deepest recesses where the natural surface of the ground is the highest, and being mounted on the loftiest ridges and highest embankments, riding above the tops of the trees, and overlooking the surrounding country, where the natural surface of the ground is the lowest—this peculiarity and this variety being occasioned by that essential requisite in a well-constructed Railway—a level line—imposing the necessity of cutting through the high lands and embanking across the low; thus in effect, presenting to the traveller all the variety of mountain and ravine in pleasing succession, whilst in reality he is moving almost on a level plane and while the natural face of the country scarcely exhibits even those slight undulations which are necessary to relieve it from tameness and insipidity.[26]

In other words, to nineteenth-century eyes, the railroad created a new, improved landscape, a real-life panorama on a global scale, incorporating real time. Small wonder that the building of the train lines sounded the death knell for the diorama fad in Paris by the 1840s. The new perspective on the world provided by this technological source of visual entertainment was described by Benjamin Gastineau in 1861 as "the synthetic philosophy of the glance"—the overview perceived as the world sweeps past the window in rapid motion, "shifting the point of view every moment . . . all visions that disappear as soon as they are seen."[27] As we have seen, Baldus's map—manifesting its ambiguous relationship to this new train vision—attempted to "fix" the afterimages left in the wake of speed. Only in the five photographs bordering the left side of the map, the five panoramic views discussed above, does Baldus suggest this new vision—in ways that are relevant to the reshaping of space in much of modernist nineteenth-century photography.

fig 6.[9]

A. Collard, from the album *Dérivation des Eaux de Vanne*, c. 1867
(Bibliothèque Historique de la Ville de Paris, Paris)

fig 6.[10]

A. Collard, from the album *Dérivation des Eaux de Vanne,* c. 1867
(Bibliothèque Historique de la Ville de Paris, Paris)

fig 6.[11]

A. Collard, *Passage des Piétons,* from the album *Viaduc d'Auteuil,* 1860s
(Bibliothèque Nationale, Paris)

And we are dealing here precisely with a *spatial* issue, which translated itself into a question of pictorial structure. Too much emphasis has been placed on content in discussions of nineteenth-century French photography, when in actual fact it is often in the form and not necessarily the content of the images that the massive changes in perceptual patterns during this period are described. Though most of the images on Baldus's map are rather hackneyed (probably in fact created by his assistants) and rarely rise above the mundane level of travel photography of the period, the five pictures on the left side at least suggest a vision that would come to fruition in the work of his contemporary, Gustave Le Gray.

As already mentioned, these five pictures, stacked one above the other, represent five separate towns along the route. Yet each of these locations is seen through the medium of the train window, and each is suitably transformed into that horizontal space that cuts across all geographic lines and levels all cultural and local differences. Each of these places—transmuted into a nonplace by the insistence of the pictorial structures—becomes one perspective, not on the town itself, but on the vision from the projectile speeding through the landscape.

Cut and framed by the window, already leveled by the construction of the tracks, these five vistas become, therefore, not photographs of the world but photographs of vision itself: less a description than almost a hallucination, a trace of what the eye sees in passing. The view from the train becomes the view from the floating head, barely linked to the environs, to the details of the particular landscape that speeds by. Whereas the rest of the photographs on the "Carte Illustré" are depictions of the exterior world and the objects and places that inhabit it, these pictures are instead its negation, and the apotheosis instead of a subjectivity created by technology and experienced continually by those observers of the "panorama" created by the train.

The images attributed to Baldus, like all panoramic photographs, are the symbolic embodiments of Gastineau's "synthetic philosophy of the glance." Certainly the most subtle and varied description of this new evanescent reality has been left to us by the master photographer Gustave Le Gray. Both André

fig 6.¹²

G. Le Gray, *Bordeaux, Inauguration of the Railroad*, n.d.
(Bibliothèque Nationale, Paris)

Jammes and Eugenia Parry Janis have remarked that the most striking visual characteristic of Le Gray's oeuvre is the insistent horizontality of his pictures.[28] They have, however, perceived this formal quality primarily as an aesthetic imperative. Perhaps it is time to broaden the scope of this perception and to understand that this vision—this consistent horizontality, projected onto the world at large—was Le Gray's attempt to visualize what Lacan and Nibelle called "space and the crowd."

One cannot, of course, make a case that Le Gray was obsessed about describing the view from the train window, any more than Baudelaire was; in fact we have, among photographs at the Bibliothèque Nationale in Paris, only one image, a documentary one, which records the opening of the railroad in Bordeaux *(fig. 6.¹²)*. Rather, Le Gray's formal and pictorial researches—and he was well known for both his theories and his technical trials in pushing the limits of camera vision—allowed him to be a medium for many of the advanced ideas of his time.

A case in point: one of the more curious of Le Gray's Parisian images, *The Entrance of the Emperor after his Coronation in the Tuileries* (1852, *fig. 6.¹³)*. Taken from the roof of the Ministry of the Marine, depicting a sweeping vision of the Place de la Concorde in Paris, the image was deeply respected by writers like Nibelle and Lacan for its emphasis on public celebrations.[29] An overview of the *place* within which thousands of people mill like ants, the photograph itself gives us little detail about the actual festival. One sees the foggy Invalides in the distance, as well as the church of St. Sulpice, with its *travaux;* one sees the fountain at Place de La Concorde spewing water in the midst of the black figures who crowd around it. But these monuments, organized as they are spatially around the dominant horizontal sweep separating land and sky in the middle of the picture plane, are hardly visualized in a hierarchic way—and nor is the information they frame. There is, in fact, by our standards, no information available here: the emperor and his party are not visible among the throng, individual Parisians have blended into the mass, the flags marking the crowd can find no patriotic significance because they are too small and too scattered

fig 6.[13]

G. Le Gray, *Place de la Concorde, Entrance of the Emperor After His Coronation in the Tuileries*, 1852 (Canadian Center for Architecture, Montreal)

to have meaning here. To our eyes, such an image is a complete failure as photojournalism.

But that was not the verdict in the 1850s, and this is significant. Clearly, the information being sought, in the days before photographically illustrated newspapers and photography schools, was of a different order, and the excitement that greeted this image alerts us to see not only its content but also its form as determinant. This is, indeed, an image of "space and the crowd," with the large empty squares, the open *places,* of the modern city taking the priority (as they did in Haussmann's urban renewal of Paris), and functioning not as particular locations but as stage sets for the ritualized activities that define modern pageantry. This crowd—anonymous, swarming, functioning simply as a mass— was the archetype of public life, the photographic statement of an activity that was to Le Gray and Lacan not a specific ceremony, a specific drama with particular players, but an icon of modernity.

In other words, on a very basic level, the point of the insistent horizontality that structures many of Le Gray's photographs was a negation of particularity; the classical balance that infuses his works was his attempt to transform the clamor of real life and real locations, like those depicted in stereographic renditions of market days or public *fêtes (figs. 6.^{14}, 6.^{15}),* into a vision whose descriptiveness was general rather than specific. Like the panoramic images bordering Baldus's map, his pictures are "destitute of prominent objects to detain the eye, or distract the attention from the charming whole." [30] Seen together, they describe the new archetypal vision of the age: the "glories of immensity," [31] embodied in Haussmann's rebuilding of Paris, hot air balloons, maps, and trains speeding through the land.

Compare, for instance, three pictures with totally different subjects: a panorama of Paris *(fig. 6.^{16}),* a seascape *(fig. 6.^{17})* and a description of a military maneuver done on assignment for Napoleon III at his Camp de Châlons *(fig. 6.^{18}).* Structurally, the three images are identical. Built around the horizon line, all three depict the sky as dominant. Taking up a bit less than two-thirds of the picture plane, it is linked to the land below on the bottom third. Within the

fig 6.[14]

H. Jouvin, *Fête de Montmartre, Place St. Pierre*, 1860s, stereocard
(Bibliothèque Nationale, Paris)

fig 6.[15]

H. Jouvin, *Group of Merchants from Les Halles*, 1860s, stereocard
(Bibliothèque Nationale, Paris)

fig 6.[16]
G. Le Gray, *The Pont du Carrousel, Paris*, c. 1856
(Canadian Center for Architecture, Montreal)

fig 6.[17]
G. Le Gray, *The Sea at Sete,* 1856–1859
(Bibliothèque Nationale, Paris)

fig 6.[18]
G. Le Gray, *Camp de Châlons, The Guard at Dawn,* 1857
(Photo Copyright Musée de l'Armée, Paris)

strict confines of this formal vision, differences emerge, but they come out of the shadows as details that never threaten to overthrow the dominance of the visual structure.

The *Pont du Carrousel,* one of a series Le Gray did in the mid-1850s, uses the bridge as its balancing point. In the foreground, most of the picture plane is taken up by the Seine, its waters still, boats lining its left bank that slopes backward into a deep space blocked from our vision by the bridge itself and the buildings in the distance that seem to bestride it. The city is small here, confined; one sees buildings lining the banks of the river, but nothing moves, everything is off to the side and quiet, echoing the deep stillness of the water. This is not a photograph, like for instance Baldus's *Panorama de la Cité* (see fig. 4.[10]), that bustles with the clamor of boats and buildings and details of the streets, hurtling backward in great haste on a diagonal. There is no action here; everything—nature, culture, monuments, spaces—is subsumed in a structural unity that takes priority over any particular content within it. Even the soft tones that pervade this pristine and, yes, serene image, with the sky blanketed by clouds that are almost indistinguishable from the general haziness, bespeak a unity that the time and space of city life will never shatter.

This emphasis on color in Le Gray's photographs is important; in works so deliberately empty, he used contrasts and subtleties of tones, as Rothko did, to create both atmosphere and drama. This is most evident, of course, in his seascapes, like the one taken at Sete in the late 1850s. In this case Le Gray's formal scaffolding is filled by a sky dense with clouds (photographed on a separate negative because of the limitations of the medium at the time) and a sea whose blackness reveals only details of waves pulling the viewer into the background of the image on a slight diagonal. This image does move into deep space; but unlike the Paris panorama, there is no perspective here, just the planes of motley color marked by a few hills on land seen at the horizon and seeming to extend indefinitely past the borders of the frame. The drama in this image is provided by the contrast of the blackness of the sea and the light of the sky, as well as by the dense clouds illuminated in the distance and hanging, somewhat menacingly, over the foreground.

In spite of its details, this picture ultimately can be read as luminous, almost weightless: the embodiment of the "glories of immensity" that provide the stage set for both human and natural life. Nowhere is this aspect of Le Gray's work more evident than in his photograph of the Camp de Châlons, part of an album (see also *fig. 6.¹⁹*) commissioned by Napoleon III in 1857. Adrien Pascal, writing about this camp in 1858, stated that "The terrain of a camp should be a theatre of practical study, independent of the aids provided by topographical maps; the glance alone should decide everything." [32] This flat, unmarked, empty land, stretching for 29,640 acres, was the perfect setting for the emperor's "splendid symbolic showplace, a sort of military Exposition Universelle" [33]— and for this photographer's panoramic vision.

The white of the sky bears down on the darkness of the ground in Le Gray's documentary image; a simple color field, this vista seems to stretch into an empty infinity in all directions. In the distance, on the ground at the horizon line, like an afterthought, we see the cavalry practicing their maneuvers. To the right are horsemen in uniform; massed together, man and beast, they are in focus just enough so that we notice their hats and some details of their tiny uniforms. They are facing more men, more soldiers, toward the left; but whereas the block of bodies, animal and human, at the right is cut by the frame so its mass seems to continue endlessly, the few horsemen mounted and scattered toward the left are separate, vague forms, indistinct in the fog, seemingly lost in the expanse of space surrounding them.

It is unclear exactly what is happening in this picture: obviously, some maneuver is taking place, a practice drill, part of the training for the French military. But Le Gray's format gives us no information about this specific event; rather, by its anonymity, its emptiness, and its theatricality, it almost forces us to see this not as a particular happening but as a more generalized ritual activity. These men are archetypes of soldiers, participating in a rite of manhood that resonates far beyond these specific males and their connection to Napoleon III and the Second Empire. The depthless space, whose fog engorges horsemen like phantoms, is Le Gray's photographic frame for modern life: that panoramic

fig 6.[19]

G. Le Gray, *Camp de Châlons,* 1857 (Photo Copyright Musée de l'Armée, Paris)

space that, by depriving us of foreground detail, allows us to perceive, dimly, the larger structures of our lives.

"The views from the windows of Europe," wrote Dolf Sternberger, "have entirely lost their dimension of depth and have become mere particles of one and the same panoramic world that stretches all around us and is, at each and every point, merely a painted surface."[34] Le Gray's photographs embody this panoramic world; space and the crowd, in these works, have metamorphosed not into a documentation of particulars but into icons that emphasize the immense generalities within which modern life takes place. These three pictures, with their identical structures, show us that "same panoramic world that stretches all around us." Whether the city, the sea, or the military, these are the painted surfaces upon which we move. Looking at Le Gray's pictures, in fact, is not unlike peering out of the window of that train from Paris to Boulogne: the landscape changes, but the frame of the picture does not. Connected to these spaces only by the mediated vision of the camera, the spectator stares into the shop window of the mind, separated by an almost immaterial barrier from the sensory experience of the real world within which he or she moves.

These are the evanescent visions that have become the stuff of modern life, the perceptions of the floating head. Yet this is the vision of evanescence—frozen: stopped in time for perusal, an attempt to grasp the living whole as it speeds by, too fast for the human eye. What Le Gray has found, however, is that once stopped, this time that is speeding by too fast reveals the same uniformity of structure that we had perceived before. The dream, once grasped, shows us not the diversity of experience but its sameness, the trivialities of difference, the immensity of the world and the smallness of our ritualized actions within it.

"We choose in nature," wrote Charles Nègre, one of Le Gray's students,[35] and art historians have seen this as the confirmation of the teacher's aesthetic intentions, the declaration of his subjective stance. In a photographic world where issues about the relationship between reality and photography were hotly debated, such an idea, of course, holds sway; but seen in a broader context, Le Gray's choice of stance links him inexorably to the social realities of his time. Le Gray's is a world in which subjective vision—the perspective, the glance, the unique regard—takes priority over any place, any event, any object on record, where nature itself becomes grist for the mill of individual sensibility. Yet it is also a world where that vision is, like the maps that delineated the railroads, mediated, systematized, closed: where the life and landscape that is perceived is, ultimately, more notable for its immense monotony than as an arena where human activity can make a difference. Lacking the obvious psychic despair of Baudelaire, Le Gray nonetheless shared the same streets with this poet, and his research into the human condition ultimately yielded the same negations. His pictures, like Baudelaire's poems, gain their power not from their documentary reality but as allegories. They, too, are afterimages trapped within the closure of the shop window of the nineteenth-century French mind.

Or maybe within the exhibition halls of Crystal Palaces, glass and steel constructions whose immaterial, transparent walls opened up vistas not unlike those seen from the trains. These new structures, originally created for the Universal Expositions, were, of course, the models for the train stations of this époque. Schivelbusch has pointed out that the early construction of railroad terminals—half palace and half factory—reflected the public's ambivalence toward the industrial character of this new means of transport. Januslike, the architectural styles of the terminals in the 1850s faced both forward and backward. The actual train halls, open sheds of glass and steel, looked forward toward the limitless, expanded space of the trains; the reception buildings, with their stone facades, closed spaces, and historicized forms, faced backward toward the comforting scale and designs of the premodern cities surrounding them. These buildings, in other words, served as *passages* from one *époque* to another—as "stimulus shields"[36] that protected the public and the urban environment from technological shock while acclimating them gradually to the immensity of railroad space. By the 1860s this public orientation was over, and consequently the dual facade of the stations became unnecessary. Industry and its concomitant spaces had permeated all aspects of both urban and conscious life and indeed become the perceptual norm.

Not surprisingly, perhaps, this acceptance of the norms of railroad vision, this "distracted" (to quote Walter Benjamin)[37] relationship to its limitless spaces, was not to be experienced by either Baudelaire or Le Gray. "Fleeing the herd where Fate had penned (him) fast," Baudelaire "took refuge in the wards of Opium" and died, his desire taking the form of hallucinatory dreams; Le Gray, on the other hand, "heart tugging like (a) balloon," jumped onto Alexander Dumas's pleasure ship bound for Egypt in 1860. "Plung(ing) deep in the Unknown to find the *new*," he remained an exile from his European homeland until his death in Cairo in 1882.[38]

Notes

I   Introduction: Time Zones

This introduction is an adaptation/expansion of an essay originally published in Paris et le Daguerreotype, *the book that accompanied an exhibition of the same title at the Musée Carnavalet in Paris in 1989.*

1   Samuel F. B. Morse, from a letter to his brother that was published in the *New York Observer*, April 9, 1839, cited in Helmut and Alison Gernsheim, *L. J. M. Daguerre* (New York: Dover Publications, 1968), pp. 89–90.

2   Official figure quoted in Louis Chevalier, *Classes Laborieuses et Classes Dangereuses à Paris, pendant la première moitié du XIXème siècle* (Paris: Hachette, 1984) p. 315.

3   Charles Baudelaire, "Loss of a Halo," in *Paris Spleen,* trans. Louise Varèse (New York: New Directions, 1970), p. 94.

4   Morse, letter to brother.

5   Roland Barthes, *Camera Lucida,* trans. Richard Howard (New York: Hill and Wang, 1981), p. 88.

6   Charles Baudelaire, "The Swan," in *Les Fleurs du Mal,* trans. Richard Howard (Boston: David R. Godine, 1983), p. 268.

7   Walter Benjamin, *Charles Baudelaire,* trans. Harry Zohn (London: Verso, 1983), p. 87.

8   M. Lachaise, *Topographie Médicale,* Paris, 1822, quoted in Chevalier, *Classes Laborieuses,* p. 270. My translation.

9   Ibid., p. 274. My translation.

10   Ibid., p. 273.

11   Figures given in David H. Pinkney, *Napoleon III and the Rebuilding of Paris* (Princeton: Princeton University Press, 1958), p. 23.

12   Maxime Du Camp, *Paris, ses organes, ses fonctions et sa vie dans la seconde moitié du XIXème siècle* (Paris: Librairie Hachette, 1895), p. 373.

13   Etienne Carjat, "L'Art du Pauvre," written in 1883 for the inauguration of the monument to Daguerre at his birthplace, Cormeilles. Quoted in Gernsheim, *L. J. M. Daguerre,* p. 128.

14   Gay Lussac, speech in the French House of Peers, July 30, 1839.

15   Barthes, *Camera Lucida,* p. 90.

16   T. J. Clark, *The Painter of Modern Life* (New York: Knopf, 1985), p. 32.

17   Balzac, quoted in Clark, ibid.

18   Barthes, *Camera Lucida,* p. 96.

19   Cited in Rob Shields, "Fancy Footwork," in *The Flâneur,* ed. Keith Tester (London: Routledge, 1994), p. 73.

20   Barthes, *Camera Lucida,* p. 88.

21   John Berger and Jean Mohr, *Another Way of Telling* (New York: Pantheon, 1982), pp. 105ff.

22   Jean Paul Sartre, *Baudelaire* (New York: New Directions, 1950), p. 63.

23   From the Goncourts's journal, November 18, 1860, quoted in Clark, *Painter of Modern Life,* p. 34.

24   Charles Baudelaire, "The Painter of Modern Life," in *The Painter of Modern Life and Other Essays,* transl. and ed. Jonathan Mayne (London: Phaidon, 1970), p. 5.

25   Susan Buck-Morss, *The Dialectics of Seeing* (Cambridge, Mass.: MIT Press, 1989), p. 186.

26   Leo Bersani, *Baudelaire and Freud* (Berkeley: University of California Press, 1977).

27   Baudelaire, "The Swan."

28   Ibid.

29   Bersani, *Baudelaire and Freud,* pp. 110–111.

30   Baudelaire, "The Swan."

II   Parisian Views

1   Charles Baudelaire, "The Eyes of the Poor," in *Paris Spleen,* trans. Louise Varèse (New York: New Directions, 1970), pp. 52–53.

2   This is a word Haussmann characteristically used throughout his *Mémoires* (Paris: Victor-Havard, 1893, 3 vols.) to describe his demolition work.

3   Marshall Berman, *All That Is Solid Melts Into Air* (New York: Simon and Schuster, 1982), p. 151.

4   For the definitive discussion of overpopulation in nineteenth-century Paris before 1848, and its effects on the city's inhabitants, see Louis Chevalier, *Classes Laborieuses et Classes Dangereuses* (Paris: Hachette, 1984).

5   Georg Simmel, *Soziologie* (Berlin: 1958), p. 486. Quoted in Walter Benjamin, *Charles Baudelaire: A Lyric Poet in the Era of High Capitalism* (London: Verso, 1983), p. 38. Translation by Harry Zohn.

6   Ibid., p. 39.

7   David H. Pinkney, *Napoleon III and the Rebuilding of Paris* (Princeton: Princeton University Press, 1972), p. 72.

8   This is a general issue elaborated in Walter Benjamin, *Charles Baudelaire*.

9   Haussmann, *Mémoires*, vol. 2, p. 53.

10   Sigfried Giedion, *Space, Time and Architecture* (Cambridge, Mass.: Harvard University Press, 1978), p. 739.

11   Pinkney, *Napoleon III*, p. 4.

12   Françoise Choay, "Pensées sur la ville, arts de la ville," in Maurice Agulhon, editor, *Histoire de la France Urbaine: la ville de l'âge industriel*, Tome 4 (Paris: Editions du Seuil, 1983), p. 165. My translation.

13   Berman, *All That Is Solid*, p. 150. For a detailed discussion of the street networks, see also P. Lavedan, *Histoire de l'Urbanisme à Paris*.

14   Pinkney, *Napoleon III*, p. 93.

15   For an excellent discussion of these changes—and their impact on the various classes and occupations of Paris—see Jean Gaillard, *Paris, La Ville 1852–1870* (Paris: Editions Honoré Champion, 1977).

16   Choay, "Pensées sur la ville," p. 168. My translation.

17   Pinkney, *Napoleon III*, p. 63.

18   Haussmann, *Mémoires*, vol. 3, pp. 74–76; and Pinkney, *Napoleon III*, p. 63.

19   Maxime Du Camp, *Paris, ses organes, ses fonctions et sa vie dans la seconde moitié du XIX siècle* (Paris: Librairie Hachette, 1893, 6 volumes), vol. 6, p. 253. Cited in Benjamin, *Charles Baudelaire*, p. 86.

20   Daly, *Etude Generale*, quoted in T. J. Clark, *The Painting of Modern Life* (New York: Knopf, 1985), p. 43.

21   Charles Yriarte, "Les Types Parisiens—les clubs" in *Paris-Guide 2*, 1867; quoted in Clark, *Painting of Modern Life*, pp. 43–44.

22   Victorien Sardou, "Maison Neuve," in *Théâtre Complet de Victorien Sardou, 9*; p. 274–275. This reference is cited in T. J. Clark, *Painting of Modern Life*, p. 42 and also in G. N. Lameyre, *Haussmann: Préfet de Paris*, pp. 281–282.

23   For further discussions of these vistas and the disengagement of monuments, see Choay, "Pensées sur la ville," and Giedion, *Space, Time and Architecture*.

24   Giedion, *Space, Time and Architecture*, p. 739.

25   For a fascinating discussion of this, see Giedion, *Space, Time and Architecture*, pp. 762–765.

26   Weston Naef speculates on this in *After Daguerre*, ex. cat. (New York: Metropolitan Museum of Art in association with Berger-Levrault, Paris, 1980), p. 17.

27   Much of my information on Blanquart-Evrard comes from Isabelle Jammes's excellent book *Blanquart-Evrard et*

les Origines de L'Edition Photographique Française (Geneve-Paris: Librairie Droz, 1981). This quote is from p. 11, my translation.

28   There is, of course, a vast literature available in both French and English on the Second Empire. For an overview of Napoleon III's life and a basic introduction to the period, see John Thompson, *Napoleon III and the Second Empire* and Alain Plessis, *De la fête impériale au mur des fédérés 1852–1871.*

29   For background on Disdéri's life and work, see Elizabeth Anne McCauley's *A. A. E. Disderi and the Carte-de-Visite Portrait Photograph* (New Haven: Yale University Press, 1985).

30   Max Kozloff, "Nadar and the Republic of Mind," in *Photography in Print,* ed. Vicki Goldberg (New York: Touchstone, 1981), p. 130.

31   Walter Benjamin, "The Work of Art in the Age of Mechanical Reproduction," in *Illuminations,* ed. Hannah Arendt, trans. Harry Zohn (New York: Schocken Books, 1969), p. 221.

32   Walter Benjamin, "A Short History of Photography," in *Classic Essays on Photography,* ed. Alan Trachtenberg, trans. P. Patton (New Haven: Leete's Island Books, 1980), p. 200.

33   Gisèle Freund, *Photography and Society* (Boston: David R. Godine, 1980), pp. 43ff.

34   This information, and much else of interest, comes from Phillipe Néagu and Jean-Jacques Poulet-Allemagny, *Anthologie D'un Patrimoine Photographique* (Paris: Caisse Nationale des Monuments Historiques et des Sites, 1980), p. 18.

35   Naef, *After Daguerre,* p. 22.

36   A. M. Vogt, *Art of the Nineteenth Century* (New York: Universe Books, 1973).

37   Naef, *After Daguerre,* p. 22.

38   Elvire Perega, "Delmaet et Durandelle, ou la rectitude des lignes," *Photographies,* no. 5, July 1984.

39   Pinkney, *Napoleon III,* p. 86.

40   Mikhail Bakhtin, "Forms of Time and the Chronotope in the Novel," 1937, quoted in J. Clifford, *The Predicament of Culture* (Cambridge, Mass.: Harvard University Press, 1988), p. 236.

41   Rob Shields, "Fancy Footwork," in ed. Keith Tester, *The Flâneur* (London: Routledge, 1994), p. 72. My thanks to Shields for ideas that were influential in the writing of this essay.

42   Ibid., p. 74.

43   Ibid., p. 68.

44   Richard Sennett, *The Fall of Public Man* (New York: Vintage Books, 1978), p. 160.

45   Baudelaire, "Windows," in *Paris Spleen,* p. 77.

46   Baudelaire, "The Painter of Modern Life," in Jonathan Mayne ed. and trans., *The Painter of Modern Life and Other Essays* (London: Phaidon, 1970), p. 18.

47   Edmond Duranty, "The New Painting," reprinted in Linda Nochlin, ed., *Impressionism and Post Impressionism: 1874–1904* (Englewood Cliffs, NJ: Prentice-Hall, 1966), p. 5.

48   Roland Barthes, "The Third Meaning," from *Image-Music-Text*, trans. S. Heath (New York: Hill and Wang, 1977).

49   Shields, "Fancy Footwork," p. 68.

50   E. A. Poe, "The Man of the Crowd," in *The Complete Tales and Poems of Edgar Allan Poe* (New York: Penguin, 1982), p. 475.

51   Benjamin mentioned this connection in several texts, most notably in "A Short History of Photography," p. 215. He was also aware of the literary connection between the dandy and the noble savage during the Second Empire, and many of the sources subsequently discussed were cited or quoted by him in his various projects, finished or unfinished, on Baudelaire and the *passages*.

52   Honoré de Balzac or Hippolyte Castine, "Concerning the Man of the Crowds," *La Semaine*, 4 October 1846; quoted by Shields, "Fancy Footwork," p. 72.

53   Baudelaire, "The Painter of Modern Life," p. 28.

54   Alexandre Dumas, *Les Mohicans de Paris* (Livre de Poche: Paris, 1973).

55   Paul Féval, *Les Habits Noirs,* 1863; quoted in Shields, "Fancy Footwork," p. 71.

56   Honoré de Balzac, from *Splendeurs et Misères des Courtisanes,* quoted in Sennett, *Fall of Public Man,* p. 154.

57   Benjamin, quoted in Shields, "Fancy Footwork," p. 71.

58   Balzac, quoted ibid., pp. 69–70.

III   Still Points in a Turning World

1   Much of the background on Marville and his work comes from *Charles Marville: Photographs of Paris at the time of the Second Empire on Loan from the Musée Carnavalet,* ex. cat., ed. Jacqueline Chambord (New York, French Institute/Alliance Française, 1981). The catalogue contains two informative essays by Maria Morris Hambourg and Marie de Thézy, to whom I am much indebted.

2   Jacques Hillairet, *Dictionnaire Historique des rues de Paris* (Paris, Les Editions de Minuit, 1963), p. 414.

3   Maria Morris Hambourg, "Charles Marville's Old Paris," in *Charles Marville,* p. 10.

4   Marie de Thézy, "Charles Marville: Photographer of Paris between 1851 and 1879," trans. Lorain Granberg, in *Charles Marville,* p. 67.

5   de Thézy, *Charles Marville,* p. 66.

6   Emile Zola, *La Bête Humaine,* trans. L. W. Tancock (Middlesex, England: Penguin Classics, 1984), pp. 54–56.

7   Richard Sennett, *The Fall of Public Man: On the Social Psychology of Capitalism* (New York: Vintage Books, 1978), p. 212.

8   François Loyer, *Paris XIXè Siècle: L'Immeuble et L'Espace Urbain,* tome 2, (Paris: Atelier Parisien d'Urbanisme, 1981), p. 17.

9   Charles Baudelaire, "In Passing," in *Les Fleurs du Mal* (Boston: David Godine, 1983), p. 97. Richard Howard's translation of the French title "A Une Passante" seems to me to be inaccurate and to mischaracterize the meaning of the poem. I would prefer a literal translation: "To a Passerby."

10   Charles Baudelaire, "The Painter of Modern Life," from *The Painter of Modern Life and Other Essays,* trans. Jonathan Mayne (London: Phaidon, 1970), pp. 28–29.

IV   On Camels and Cathedrals

1   Both the Viollet-le-Duc quote and the preceding information about the history of architectural preservation can be found in Joel A. Herschmann and William W. Clark, *Un Voyage Hèliographique à Faire: The Mission of 1851,* ex. cat. (New York: Godwin-Ternbach Museum at Queens College, 1981).

2   Quoted in Pierre-Marie Auzas, *Les Grandes Heures de Notre-Dame de Paris* (Paris: Editions Tel, 1951), p. 36. My translation.

3   This quote, and background on Quatremère de Quincy, can be found in Pierre Lavedan, *Histoire de l'Urbanisme à Paris* (Paris: Diffusion Hachette, 1975), p. 312. My translation.

4   Sigfried Giedion, *Space, Time and Architecture* (Cambridge, Mass.: Harvard University Press, 1978), p. 739.

5   François Loyer, *Paris XIXe Siècle: L'Immmeuble et L'Espace Urbain* (Paris: Atelier Parisien d'Urbanisme, 1981), p. 111. My translation.

6   This issue, and its significance for art and perception in the nineteenth century, is discussed in Jonathan Crary's *Techniques of the Observer* (Cambridge, Mass.: MIT Press, 1990), p. 52.

7   Information on the historical background of panoramas in general is available in two exhibition catalogues: *Panoramania* by Ralph Hyde, from the Barbican Art Gallery in London in 1989, and *Sehsucht* from the Kunst- und Ausstellungshalle der Bundesrepublik Deutschland in Bonn in 1993. More background on French panoramic photography can be found in Philippe Néagu and Jean-Jacques Poulet-Allemagny, *Anthologie d'un Patrimoine Photographique* (Paris: Caisse Nationale des Monuments Historiques et des Sites, 1980), pp. 130–133.

V   Souvenirs

1   Friedrich von Raumer, *Briefe aus Paris und Frankreich im Jahre 1830* (Liepzig: 1831), vol. 2, p. 127. In Walter Benjamin, *Charles Baudelaire: A Lyric Poet in the Era of High Capitalism,* trans. Harry Zohn (London: Verso, 1983), p. 84.

2   Victor Hugo, "A l'Arc de Triomphe," in *Victor Hugo, Oeuvres Complètes* (Paris: La Librairie Collendorf, 1909), pp. 378–392.

3   Maxime Du Camp, *Paris, ses organes, ses fonctions et sa vie dans la seconde moitié du XIXeme siècle* (Paris: Librairie Hachette, 1875).

4   Paul Bouget, "Discours académique du 13 juin 1895: Succession à Maxime Du Camp" quoted in Benjamin, *Charles Baudelaire,* p. 86.

5   Théophile Gautier, "Mosaique des Ruines," in *Paris et Les Parisiens au XIX siècle: Moeurs, arts et monuments* (Paris: Morizot, 1856).

6   Edmond About, "Dans les ruines" in Louis Ulbach, ed., *Paris-Guide par les principaux écrivains et artistes de la France* (Paris: Librairie Internationale, 1867).

7   For a discussion of the transformation of Paris, see David Pinkney, *Napoleon III and the Rebuilding of Paris* (Princeton: Princeton University Press, 1972).

8   Maxime Du Camp, *Paris,* vol. 6, p. 253. The translation is mine, and from here on, if no other name is specified, translations are my own.

9   Ibid., p. 266.

10   Benjamin, *Charles Baudelaire,* p. 82.

11   Louis Blanc, "Le Vieux Paris," originally published in Louis Ulbach, ed., *Paris-Guide.* Reprinted in a new, abridged edition of this book, Corinne Verdet, ed., *Paris Guide par les principaux écrivains et artistes de la France* (Paris: Editions La Découverte, 1983), pp. 15–19.

12   Ibid., p. 16.

13   Ibid., p. 17.

14   Ibid.

15   Ibid.

16   Ibid.

17   Ibid., p. 18.

18   For further information on this subject, see chapter 2. For a discussion of Blanquart-Evrard's contribution to the mass reproduction and marketing of photographs, see Isabelle Jammes's excellent book, *Blanquart-Evrard et les origines de l'édition photographique française* (Genève, Paris: Librairie Droz, 1981).

19   Joseph Joubert, *Pensées Précédés de sa correspondance* (Paris: 1883), vol. 2, p. 267.

20   Roland Barthes, *Camera Lucida* (New York: Hill and Wang, 1981), p. 90.

21   For a valuable discussion of this aspect of Proust's work, see Roger Shattuck, *Proust's Binoculars* (Princeton: Princeton University Press, 1983).

22   Edmond and Jules de Goncourt, quoted in T. J. Clark, *The Painting of Modern Life: Paris in the Art of Manet and His Followers* (New York: Knopf, 1985), p. 34.

23   Nadar, "Le Dessus et le dessous de Paris," in Verdet, ed., *Paris-Guide,* p. 171.

24   T. J. Clark, *Painting of Modern Life,* pp. 67, 69.

25   Charles Baudelaire, *Intimate Journals,* trans. Christopher Isherwood (San Francisco: City Lights Books, 1983), p. 79.

26   Nadar, *A Terre et en l'air: Mémoires du Géant* (Paris: E. Dentus, 1865).

27   Benjamin, *Charles Baudelaire,* p. 162.

28   Marshall Berman, *All That is Solid Melts into Air* (New York: Simon and Schuster, 1982), pp. 13–14.

29   Nigel Gosling, *Nadar* (New York: Knopf, 1976) and André Jammes, introduction to *Nadar* (Paris: Delpire Editeur, 1982).

30   Quoted in Gosling, *Nadar,* p. 37.

31   Charles Baudelaire, "The Painter of Modern Life" in Charles Baudelaire, *The Painter of Modern Life and Other Essays,* trans. and ed. Jonathan Mayne (London and New York: Phaidon, 1970), p. 5.

32   Gosling, *Nadar,* p. 13.

33   Walter Benjamin, "The Work of Art in the Age of Mechanical Reproduction," in Hannah Arendt, ed., *Illuminations* (New York: Schocken, 1969), p. 226.

34   Most of the background information on burial practices here comes from Philippe Ariès's excellent books *The Hour of Death* (New York: Knopf, 1981) and *Western Attitudes Toward Death* (Baltimore: Johns Hopkins University Press, 1974).

35   Quoted in Philippe Ariès, "Contribution à l'étude du culte des morts à l'époque contemporaine," in Ariès, *Essais sur l'histoire de la mort,* (Paris: Seuil, 1975), p. 153.

36   Ibid., p. 151.

37   Ibid., p. 153.

38   Ibid., p. 155.

39   Charles Kunstler, *Paris Souterrain* (Paris: Flammarion, 1953), p. 107.

40   Victor Hugo, *Les Misérables,* trans. Lee Fahnestock and Norman MacAfee (New York: Signet Classics, 1987), p. 1261.

41   Jean Prinet and Antoinette Dilasser, *Nadar* (Paris: Librairie Armand Colin, 1966), p. 141.

42   All information about Nadar's artificial light experiments and patents is from ibid., p. 139.

43   Nadar, *Quand J'étais photographe* (Plan de la Tour (Var): Editions d'Aujourd-hui, 1979), p. 128.

44 Charles Baudelaire, "The Swan," in *Les Fleurs du Mal,* trans. Richard Howard (Boston: David R. Godine, 1983), p. 90.

45 Hugo, *Les Misérables,* pp. 1276–1305.

46 Ibid., p. 1259.

47 Kunstler, *Paris Souterrain,* p. 27.

48 Hugo, *Les Misérables,* p. 1265.

49 René Suttel, *Catacombes et Carrières de Paris* (Paris: Editions S.E.H.D.A.C.S, 1986), p. 59.

50 Richard A. Etlin, *The Architecture of Death* (Cambridge, Mass.: MIT Press, 1984), p. 146.

51 From Nadar, *Quand J'étais photographe;* quoted in Philippe Néagu, *Le Paris Souterrain de Félix Nadar* (Paris: Caisse Nationale des Monuments Historiques et des Sites, 1982), p. 7.

52 This and all subsequent unfootnoted quotes on the catacombs are from Nadar, "Le Dessus et le dessous de Paris," pp. 156–159.

53 Etlin, *Architecture of Death,* p. 159.

54 This and all subsequent unfootnoted quotes about the sewers are from Nadar, "Le Dessus et le dessous de Paris," p. 162.

55 Hugo, *Les Misérables,* p. 1261.

56 Ibid., p. 1276.

57 Ibid., p. 1270.

58 Ibid., p. 1269.

59 Background information on the construction of the sewers under Haussmann can be found in Pinkney, *Napoleon III,* pp. 127–145.

60 Hugo, *Les Misérables,* op. cit., p. 1259.

61 Kunstler, *Paris Souterrain,* p. 58 and back cover.

62 Hugo, *Les Misérables,* op. cit., p. 1270.

63 Nadar, *Mémoires du Géant,* p. 513.

64 Nadar, "Le Dessus," p. 172. Hereafter, all Nadar quotes without notes about Paris or the skies are from this essay, pp. 164–172. A note of interest: Nadar, like his friend Victor Hugo, saw in this opening up of the skies the possibility for democracy and equality, within and between nations, because borders would no longer make sense in the wake of flying machines.

65 Etienne Louis Boullée, "Architecture: Essay on Art," reprinted in Helen Rosenau, *Boullée and Visionary Architecture,* trans. Sheila de Vallée (New York: Harmony Books, 1976), p. 107.

66 Berman, *All That Is Solid,* p. 150.

67 Baudelaire, "The Swan," p. 91.

68 Barthes, *Camera Lucida,* p. 91.

VI Voyages without Steam or Sail

1 Charles Baudelaire, "The Swan" in *Les Fleurs du Mal (The Flowers of Evil)*, trans. Richard Howard (David Godine: Boston, 1983), pp. 90 (English) and 286 (French).

2 Baudelaire, "The Sun," ibid., 87 and 265.

3 Joseph von Eichendorff, *Werke* (Munich, 1970), vol. 2, p. 895.

4 Walter Benjamin, "The Work of Art in the Age of Mechanical Reproduction," in Hannah Arendt, ed., *Illuminations* (Schocken: New York, 1969), p. 222.

5 Jonathan Crary, *Techniques of the Observer* (Cambridge, Mass.: MIT Press, 1990), p. 113.

6 Ruskin, *The Complete Works,* vol. 8, p. 159, quoted in Wolfgang Schivelbusch, *The Railway Journey* (Berkeley: The University of California Press, 1986), p. 54.

7 Ibid., p. 64.

8 Quoted in Schivelbusch, ibid.

9 R. W. Emerson, from his *Journals,* 7 February 1843, quoted in Schivelbusch, ibid., p. 52.

10 Heinrich Heine, *Lutezia,* pt. 2, Elster edition, vol. 6, page 360.

11 Ibid.

12 Charles Baudelaire, "The Painter of Modern Life," in *The Painter of Modern Life and Other Essays,*" trans. and ed. Jonathan Mayne (London: Phaidon, 1965), p. 9.

13 Baudelaire, *Les Fleurs du Mal*, pp. 151–157. All subsequent unmarked quotes are from the poem "Travelers." The literal translation of the French title, "Le Voyage," (The Voyage) differs from Howard's translation.

14 Emile Zola, *Au Bonheur des Dames* (Paris: Fasquelle, 1984).

15 Constantin Pecqueur, *Economie Sociale* (Paris, 1839), vol. 1, p. 26.

16 Jean Baudrillard, "The Precession of Simulacra," in *Art After Modernism,* ed. Brian Wallis (New York and Boston: New Museum and David R. Godine Publishers, 1984), p. 253.

17 Erwin Straus, *The Primary World of the Senses* (New York: MacMillan, 1963), p. 320.

18 Malcolm Daniels, "Edouard Baldus, Les Albums du Chemin de fer du Nord," *La Recherche Photographique,* February 1990.

19 Daniels, ibid., p. 86. Daniels, in his essay, discusses the six versions of the album in detail. All statements in this text refer to the version of the album, created for a Mr. G. Dalton, which is in the Bibliothèque Nationale in Paris.

20 Jules Claretie, *Voyages d'un Parisien* (Paris, 1865), p. 4.

21   Schivelbusch, *Railway Journey*, p. 63.

22   Baudelaire, "The Painter of Modern Life," pp. 1–40.

23   These ideas come from Lacan, "Le Retour du Prince-President," (*La Lumière*, October 30, 1852, p. 179); "La Photographie et les Fêtes Publiques" (*La Lumière*, September 23, 1854); and Nibelle, from an article published in the same magazine on August 27, 1854.

24   *The Sociology of Georg Simmel*, ed. Kurt M. Wolf (Glencoe, Ill., 1950), p. 410.

25   Schivelbusch, *Railway Journey*, p. 62.

26   Francis Lieber, *The Stranger in America* (London, 1834), vol. 2, pp. 1–2.

27   Benjamin Gastineau, *La Vie en Chemin de Fer* (Paris: 1861), p. 31.

28   Eugenia Parry Janis, *The Photography of Gustave Le Gray* (Chicago: The Art Institute of Chicago and the University of Chicago Press, 1987), p. 21 and elsewhere.

29   See Lacan's review of this picture in *La Lumière* in 1852, op. cit.

30   Matthew Ward, *English Items* (New York, 1853), pp. 71–72.

31   Janis, *Le Gray*, op. cit. p. 145.

32   Adrien Pascal, from "Introduction" to Charles Bousquet, *Le Garde Imperiale au Camp de Châlons* (Paris: Imprimerie et Librairie Militaire de Blot, 1858), pp. 144–145. This quote, and much information about the camp itself and the life within it, can be found in Janis, *Le Gray*, pp. 84–99.

33   Ibid., p. 86.

34   Dolf Sternberger, *Panorama of the Nineteenth Century* (Hamburg, 1955), p. 57; English version trans. Joachim Neugroschel (New York: Urizen Books, 1977).

35   Quoted in Janis, *Le Gray*, p. 33.

36   Schivelbusch, *Railway Journey*, p. 175.

37   Benjamin "The Work of Art," p. 240.

38   All quotes are from "Travelers" by Charles Baudelaire, *Les Fleurs du Mal*, op. cit.; information about Le Gray's sojourn with Dumas, whose boat never made it to Egypt, and subsequent travels and life in Egypt, can be found in Janis, *Le Gray*, pp. 125ff.

Selected Bibliography

Photography

After Daguerre: Masterworks of French Photography, 1848–1900 from the Bibliothèque Nationale. Ex. cat. Metropolitan Museum of Art, with essays by Jean-Pierre Sequin and Weston Naef; catalogue by Bernard Marbot. New York: Metropolitan Museum, 1980.

Avice, Jean-Paul. *Les Ciels de Paris.* Paris: Agence Culturelle de Paris, 1994.

Besson, George. *Un Siècle de Technique: Etablissements Braun et Cie.* Colmar: Braun et Cie, 1948.

Barthes, Roland. *Camera Lucida.* New York: Hill and Wang, 1981.

Benjamin, Walter. "A Short History of Photography." Trans. Phil Patton. *Artforum* Feb. 1977, pp. 46–51.

Benjamin, Walter. "The Work of Art in the Age of Mechanical Reproduction." Trans. Harry Zohn. In *Illuminations,* ed. Hannah Arendt. New York: Schocken Books, 1969, pp. 217–252.

Borhan, Pierre. *Charles Marville: Les Vespasiennes.* Paris: Tête d'Affiche, 1994.

Borcomon, James. *Charles Nègre.* Ex. cat. National Gallery of Canada. Ottawa: 1976.

Brettell, Richard et al. *Paper and Light: The Calotype in France and Great Britain 1839–1870.* Ex. cat. Museum of Fine Arts, Houston/Art Institute of Chicago. Boston: Godine, 1984.

Buerger, Janet. *The Era of the French Calotype.* Ex. cat. International Museum of Photography at George Eastman House. Rochester: 1982.

Cabaud, Michel. *Paris et Les Parisiens Sous le Second Empire.* Paris: Belfond, 1982.

Etienne Carjat 1828–1906. Ex. cat. Musée Carnavalet. Paris: 1982.

Cheronnet, L. *Paris Tel Qu'il Fut.* Paris: Editions Tel, 1951.

Christ, Yvan. *L'Age D'Or de la Photographie*. Paris: Vincent, Frèal et Cie., 1965.

Colson, R. *Mémoires Originaux des Créateurs de la Photographie*. Paris: G. Carve and C. Naud, 1898.

Crary, Jonathan. *Techniques of the Observer*. Cambridge, Mass.: MIT Press, 1990.

Daniels, Malcolm et al. *The Photographs of Edouard Baldus*. Ex.cat. Metropolitan Museum of Art. New York, 1994.

De Thézy, Marie. *Charles Marville*. Paris: Hazan, 1994.

De Thézy, Marie. "Charles Marville et Haussmann." In *Monuments Historiques: Photographie et Architecture* no. 110. Paris: CNMHS, n.d.

De Thézy, Marie. *Charles Marville: Paris Disparu*. Paris: Tête d'Affiche, 1994.

De Thézy, Marie. *Charles Marville: Réverbères*. Paris: Tête d'Affiche, 1993.

D'Eugny, Anne. *Au Temps de Baudelaire, Guys et Nadar*. Paris: Les Editions du Chêne, 1945.

Didi Huberman, Georges. *L'invention de l'Hysterie*. Paris: Macula, 1982.

Du Camp, Maxime. *Egypte, Syrie, Palestine, Nubie*, Tomes 1 et 2. Paris: Gide et Baudry, 1852.

English, Donald. *Political Uses of Photography in the Third French Republic,* *1871–1914*. Ann Arbor, Mich.: UMI Research Press, 1984.

Fargue, L. P. *Dans Les Rues de Paris au Temps des Fiacres*. Paris: Les Editions du Chêne, 1950.

de Fenoyl, Pierre. *Chefs d'Oeuvre des Photographes Anonymes du XIXème Siècle*. Paris: Hachette, 1982.

Figuier, Louis. *La Photographie au Salon de 1859*. Paris: Hachette, 1860.

Figuier, Louis. *Les Applications Nouvelles de la Science à l'Industrie et Aux Arts en 1855*. Paris: Victor Masson/Langlois et Leclerq, 1856.

Freund, Gisèle. *Photography and Society*. Boston: Godine, 1980.

Freund, Gisèle. *Photographie en France au 19ème Siècle*. Paris: A. Monnier, 1936.

Frizot, Michel, ed. *La Nouvelle Histoire de la Photographie*. Paris: Bordas, 1994.

Galassi, Peter. *Before Photography*. Ex.cat. Museum of Modern Art. New York: 1981.

Gautrand, Jean-Claude, and Michel Frizot. *Hippolyte Bayard: Naissance de l'Image Photographique*. Amiens: Trois Cailloux, 1986.

Gimon, Gilbert. "Humbert de Molard 1800–1874." *Prestige de la Photographie* no. 5, (Nov. 1978): 66–95; and part 2, no. 7 (Aug. 1979): 3–35.

Gimon, Gilbert. "Jules Itier: Daguerreo-types de Chine et d'Egypte." *Prestige de la Photographie* no. 8 (Dec. 1979–Jan. 1980): 80–99; part 2, no. 9 (Apr. 1980).

Gosling, Nigel, *Nadar.* New York: Knopf, 1976.

Le Grand Oeuvre: Photographies des Grands Travaux 1860–1900. Photo Poche book with essay by Jean Desjours. Paris: Centre National de la Photographie, 1983.

Greaves, Roger. *Nadar.* Paris: Flammarion, 1980.

Heilbrun, Françoise, and Philippe Néagu. *Charles Nègre: Photographe, 1820–1880.* Ex. cat. Arles, Musée Réattu and Paris, Musée de Luxembourg. Paris: Dossier d'Orsay 2, 1980.

Heilbrun, Françoise, Philippe Néagu, et al. *Nadar.* Ex. cat. Paris, Musée d'Orsay and New York, Metropolitan Museum of Art. Paris: Réunion des Musées Nationaux, 1994.

Une Invention du XIXème Siècle: La Photographie. Ex. cat. Collections de la Société Française de Photographie. Paris: Bibliothèque Nationale, 1976.

Jammes, André, and Robert Sobieszek. *French Primitive Photography.* Ex. cat. Philadelphia Museum of Art. Millerton, N.Y.: Aperture, 1969.

Jammes, André. *Nadar.* Photo Poche, Fondation Nationale de la Photographie. Paris: Delpire, 1982.

Jammes, Isabelle. *Albums Photographiques edités par Blanquart-Evrard.* Paris: Kodak-Pathé, 1978.

Jammes, Isabelle. *Blanquart-Evrard et les Origines de l'Edition Photographique Française.* Genève-Paris: Librairie Droz, 1981.

Janis, Eugenia Parry, and A. Jammes. *The Art of the French Calotype.* Princeton: Princeton University Press, 1983.

Janis, Eugenia Parry, and Josiane Sartre. *Henri Le Secq: Photographe de 1850–1860.* Catalogue raisonné de la collection de la Bibliothèque des Arts Décoratifs, Musée des Arts Décoratifs. Paris: Flammarion, 1986.

Janis, Eugenia Parry. "The Man on the Tower of Notre-Dame: New Light on Henri Le Secq." *Image* 19, no. 4 (Dec. 1976): 13–25.

Janis, Eugenia Parry. *The Photography of Gustave Le Gray.* Ex. cat. The Art Institute of Chicago and the Musée d'Orsay, Paris. Chicago: University of Chicago Press, 1987.

Janis, Eugenia Parry. "To Still the Telling Lens: Observations on the Art of the French Calotype." *The Creative Eye: Occasional Papers of the Connecticut Humanities Council* no. 4, 1981.

Kempf, Christian. *Adolphe Braun, 1812–1877*. Colmar: Editions Lucigraphie/Valbor, 1994.

Kozloff, Max. "Nadar and the Republic of Mind." *Artforum* (Sept. 1976): 28–39.

Krauss, Rosalind. "Tracing Nadar." *October* no. 5 (Summer 1978): 29–47.

Lacan, Ernest. *Esquisses Photographiques*. Paris: Grassart, 1856.

La Lumière: Journal non-politique. Paris, 1851–1867.

Lécuyer, Raymond. *Histoire de la Photographie*. Paris: Baschet et Cie., 1945.

Lerebours, N. P. *Excursions Daguerriennes*. Paris: 1843.

Charles Marville: Photographe de Paris de 1851 à 1879. Essay by Marie de Thézy. Ex. cat. Bibliothèque Historique de la Ville de Paris. Paris: 1980.

Charles Marville: Photographs of Paris from the Musée Carnavalet. Essays by Maria Morris Hambourg and Marie de Thézy. Ex. cat. French Institute/Alliance Française. New York: 1981.

McCauley, Elizabeth Anne. *A. A. E. Disdéri and the Carte-de-Visite Portrait Photograph*. New Haven: Yale University Press, 1985.

McCauley, Elizabeth Anne. "Adolphe Eugène Disdéri." *Prestige de la Photographie* no. 5 (Nov. 1978): 4–47.

McCauley, Elizabeth Anne. "Caricature and Photography in Second Empire Paris." *Art Journal* 43, no. 4 (Winter 1983): 355–360.

McCauley, Elizabeth Anne. *Industrial Madness*. New Haven: Yale University Press, 1994.

McCauley, Elizabeth Anne. "The Photographic Adventure of Maxime Du-Camp." In *Perspectives on Photography*, edited by David Oliphant and Thomas Zigal. Austin: University of Texas, Humanities Research Center, 1982.

Miguel, Pierre. *Le Second Empire*. Paris: André Barret, 1979.

Nadar. *Charles Baudelaire Intime*. Orne: Obsidiane, 1985.

Nadar. *Le Paris Souterrain de Félix Nadar*. Ex. cat. Caisse Nationale des Monuments Historiques et des Sites. Paris: 1982.

Nadar. *Quand J'Etais Photographe*. Paris: Editions d'Aujourd'hui, 1979.

Nadar. *A Terre et en L'Air: Mémoires du Géant*. Paris: E. Dentu, 1865.

Néagu, Philippe, and Jean-Jacques Poulet-Allamagny. *Anthologie d'un Patrimoine Photographique*. Paris: Caisse Nationale des Monuments Historiques et des Sites, 1980.

Néagu, Philippe, and Françoise Heilbrun. "Etude: Baldus, Paysages, Architectures." *Photographies* numéro 1 (Printemps 1983): 56–77.

Néagu, Philippe. *La Mission Héliographique: Photographies de 1851.* Paris: Direction des Musées de France, 1980.

Néagu, Philippe. *1851: La Mission Héliographique,* supplement to the revue *Photographies,* no. 1, 1984, pp. 11–21.

Néagu, Philippe, and J. J. Poulet-Allamagny, ed. *Nadar.* Photographies, Tome 1; Dessins et Ecrits, Tome 2. Paris: Arthur Hubschmid, 1979.

Nesbit, Molly. *Atget's Seven Albums.* New Haven: Yale University Press, 1992.

Nori, Claude. *French Photography from its Origins to the Present.* New York: Pantheon, 1979.

Perego, Elvire. "Delmaet et Durandelle ou La Rectitude des Lignes." *Photographies* no. 5 (July 1984): 54–73.

Prinet, Jean, and Antoinette Dilasser. *Nadar.* Paris: Librairie Armand Colin, 1960.

Rambert, Louis. "Le Dubroni: un appareil à developpement instantané." *Prestige de la Photographie* no. 1 (June 1977): 96–117.

Ramstedt, Nils Walter Jr. "The Photographs of Gustave Le Gray" Ph.D. diss., University of California, Santa Barbara. Ann Arbor, Mich.: University Microfilms International, 1981.

Reynaud, Françoise et al. *Paris et le Daguerreotype.* Ex. cat. Musée Carnavalet. Paris: Paris Musées, 1989.

Rouillé, André. *L'Empire de la Photographie.* Paris: Le Sycomore, 1982.

Rouillé, André. "Les Images Photographiques du Monde du Travail Sous le Second Empire." *Actes de la Recherces en Sciences Socials* no. 54 (Sept. 1984).

Rouillé, André. *La Photographie en France, Textes et Controverses: Une Anthologie, 1816–1871.* Paris: Macula, 1989.

Sagne, Jean. *L'Atelier du Photographe 1840–1940.* Paris: Presses de la Renaissance, 1984.

Sagne, Jean. "Eugène Delacroix et la Photographie." *Prestige de la Photographie,* no. 9 (Apr. 1980): 62–85.

Scharf, Aaron. *Art and Photography.* Baltimore: Penguin Books, 1974.

Schwarz, Heinrich. *Art and Photography: Forerunners and Influences.* Rochester: Visual Studies Workshop, 1985.

Le Second Empire Vous Regard, issue 53 of *Le Point: Revue Artistique et Litteraire,* (Jan. 1958).

Sekula, Allan. "The Body and the Archive." *October* 39 (Winter 1986): 3–64.

Solomon-Godeau, Abigail. "The Legs of the Countess." *October* 39 (Winter 1986): 65–108.

Un Voyage Héliographique à Faire: The Mission of 1851. Ex. cat., Godwin-Ternbach Museum at Queens College. New York, 1981.

Tyl, Pierre. *Adolphe Braun: Photographe.* Mémoire de Maitrise d'Histoire. Université de Strasbourg II, 1982.

Tyl, Pierre. "Mayer et Pierson." *Prestige de la Photographie* no. 6 (Apr. 1979): 4–31; no. 7 (Aug. 1979): 36–63.

Wey, Francis. "Un Voyage Héliographique à Faire." *La Lumière,* Paris, April 23, 1851.

Younger, Daniel, ed. *Multiple Views: Logan Grant Essays on Photography 1983–1989.* Albuquerque: University of New Mexico Press, 1991.

Haussmann, Paris Architecture, and City Planning

Agulhon, Maurice. *La Ville de l'Age Industriel,* Tome 4 de *l'Histoire de la France Urbaine,* sous la direction de George Duby. Paris: Editions de Seuil, 1983.

Alphand, Adolphe. *Les Promenades de Paris.* Paris: 1867–1873.

Anderson, Stanford, ed. *On Streets.* Cambridge, Mass.: MIT Press, 1986.

Baedeker, Karl. *Paris and Its Environs.* Leipsic: Baedeker Guidebooks; English edition, London, 1884.

Benevolo, Leonardo. *The History of the City.* Trans. Geoffrey Culverwell. Cambridge, Mass.: MIT Press, 1980.

Benevolo, Leonardo. *The Origins of Modern Town Planning.* Trans. Judith Landry. Cambridge, Mass.: MIT Press, 1967.

Benjamin, Walter. *Paris: Capitale du XIXè Siècle.* Paris: Les Editions du Cerf, 1989.

Bercé, Françoise, and Bruno Foucart. *Viollet-le-Duc: Architect, Artist, Master of Historic Preservation.* Washington, D.C.: The Trust for Museum Exhibitions, 1988.

Berty, A. *Histoire Générale de Paris I and Topographie Historique du Vieux Paris,* 6 volumes. Paris: Imprimerie Impériale, 1866.

Bowie, Karen, ed. *Les Grandes Gares Parisiennes au XIXème Siècle.* Paris: La

Délégation à l'Action Artistique de la Ville de Paris, 1987.

Briggs, Asa. *Iron Bridge to Crystal Palace.* London: Thames and Hudson, Ltd., 1979.

Buck-Morss, Susan. *The Dialectics of Seeing: Walter Benjamin and the Arcades Project.* Cambridge, Mass.: MIT Press, 1989.

Caceres, C. G., and Marie-Ange de Pierredon. *Les Décors des Boutiques Parisiennes.* Paris: Délégation à l'Action Artistique de la Ville de Paris, 1987.

Cain, Georges. *Nouvelles Promenades dans Paris.* Paris: Flammarion, n.d.

Cerdá, Ildefonso. *Théorie Générale de l'Urbanisation.* Paris: Editions du Seuil, 1979.

Chapman, J. *The Life and Times of Baron Haussmann.* London: Weidenfeld and Nicolson, 1957.

Chemetov, Paul, and Bernard Marrey. *Architectures, Paris, 1848–1914.* Paris: Dunod, 1980.

Choay, Françoise. *The Modern City: Planning in the 19th Century.* New York: Braziller, 1969.

Christ, Yvan. *Les Metamorphoses de Paris.* Paris: A. Balland, 1967.

Christ, Yvan. *Les Nouvelles Metamorphoses de Paris.* Paris: A. Balland, 1976.

Couperie, Pierre. *Paris Through the Ages.* Trans. Marilyn Low. New York: Braziller, 1968.

Daly, César. *L'Architecture Privée au XIXè Siècle.* Paris: Ducker et Cie. 3 vols.: 1st series 1864, 2nd series, 1872, 3rd series 1877.

Des Cars, Jean. *Haussmann: La Gloire du 2nd Empire.* Paris: Librairie Academique Perrin, 1978.

Des Cars, Jean, and Pierre Pinon. *Paris: Haussmann.* Paris: Picard, 1991.

Drexler, Arthur. *The Architecture of the Ecole des Beaux-Arts.* Ex. cat. Museum of Modern Art. New York, 1977.

Etlin, Richard A. *The Architecture of Death: The Transformation of the Cemetery in 18th-Century Paris.* Cambridge, Mass.: MIT Press, 1987.

Evenson, Norma. *Paris: A Century of Change 1878–1978.* New Haven: Yale University Press, 1979.

Ferry, Jules. *Comptes Fantastiques d'Haussmann.* Paris: Armand le Chevalier, 1868.

Forster, Kurt S. "Schinkel's Panoramic Planning of Central Berlin." *Modulus* no. 16, n.d., pp. 5–10.

Fournel, Victor. *Ce qu'on Voit dans les Rues de Paris.* Paris: Adolphe Delahayes, 1858.

Fournel, Victor. *Paris Nouveau et Paris Futur.* Paris: Le Coffre fils et Cie., 1868.

Gaillard, Jean. *Paris: La Ville 1852–1870.* Paris: Editions Honoré Champion, 1877.

Giedion, Siegfried. *Space, Time and Architecture.* Cambridge, Mass.: Harvard University Press, 1978.

Louis Girard. *La Politique des Travaux Publics du 2nd Empire.* Paris: Librairie Armand Colin, 1951.

Les Grands Boulevards. Ex. cat. Musée Carnavalet. Paris, 1985.

Gutkind, E. A. *International History of City Development.* Vol. 5, *Urban Development in Western Europe: France and Belgium.* New York: Free Press, 1970.

Hales, Peter Bacon. *Silver Cities.* Philadelphia: Temple University Press, 1984.

Harvey, David. *The Urbanization of Capital.* Baltimore: Johns Hopkins, 1985.

Harvey, David. *Consciousness and the Urban Experience.* Baltimore: Johns Hopkins, 1985.

Haussman, G. E. *Histoire Générale de Paris: Collection des Documents Fondée Avec l'Approbation de L'Empereur par M. le Baron Haussmann et publiée sous les auspices du Conseil Municipal.* Paris: Imprimerie Impériale, 1866.

Haussman, G. E. *Mémoires du Baron Haussmann,* 3 vols. Paris: Victor-Havard, 1893.

Hillairet, Jacques. *Dictionnaire Historique des Rues de Paris.* Paris: Editions de Minuit, 1963.

Hillairet, Jacques. *Connaissance du Vieux Paris.* Paris: Editions Princesse, 1956.

Hitchcock, Henry Russell. *Architecture: 19th and 20th Centuries.* Pelican History of Art Series. Baltimore: Penguin, 1971.

Joanne, Adolphe. *Le Guide Parisien.* Paris: Librairie L. Hachette et Cie., 1863.

Kunstler, Charles. *Paris Souterrain.* Paris: Flammarion, 1953.

Lameyre, Gérard. *Haussmann, Prefet de Paris.* Paris: Flammarion, 1958.

Lavedan, Pierre. *Histoire de l'Urbanisme,* 3 volumes. Paris: Henri Laurens, 1959.

Lavedan, Pierre. *Histoire de l'Urbanisme à Paris.* Paris: Imprimerie Municipale, 1975.

Lemoine, Bertrand. *Gustave Eiffel.* Paris: F. Hazan, 1984.

Lemoine, Bertrand. *Les Passages Couverts.* Paris: Delegation à l'Action Artistique de la Ville de Paris, 1989.

Leniaud, Jean Michel. *Viollet-le-Duc.* Paris: Menges, 1989.

Loyer, François. *Paris XIXè Siècle: L'Immeuble et l'Espace Urbain*. Paris: Atelier Parisien d'Urbanisme, 1981.

Loyer, François. *Paris XIXè Siècle: L'Immeuble et la Rue*. Paris: Editions Hazan, 1987.

Loyer, François. *Le Siècle de l'Industrie*. Paris: Skira, 1983.

Lynch, Kevin. *The Image of the City*. Cambridge, Mass.: MIT Press, 1968.

Malet, H. *Le Baron Haussmann et la Renovation de Paris*. Paris: Les Editions Municipale, 1973.

Marrey, Bernard, et Paul Chemetov. *Architectures, Paris, 1848–1914*. Ex. cat. Secretaire d'Etat à la Culture avec participation de la Caisse Nationale des Monuments Historiques et des Sites et la Section Française de l'ICOMAS. Paris: 1976.

Mellot, Philippe. *Paris Sens Dessus-Dessous*. Mantes la Jolie: Editions Michele Trinekvel, 1993.

Métropolitain. Ex. cat. et actes du colloque, Bibliothèque Historique de la Ville de Paris. Paris, 1988.

Mignot, Claude. *L'Architecture au XIXè Siècle*. Fribourg, Switzerland: Editions du Moniteur, 1983.

Missac, Pierre. *Walter Benjamin's Passages*. Cambridge, Mass.: MIT Press, 1995.

de Moncan, Patrice. *Baltard: Les Halles de Paris*. Paris: Les Editions de L'Observatoire, 1994.

de Moncan Patrice, and Christian Mahonet. *Le Paris du Baron Haussmann*. Paris: Editions Seesam, 1991.

Morizet, A. *Du Vieux Paris au Paris Moderne*. Paris: Hachette, 1932.

Mumford, Lewis. *The City in History*. New York: Harcourt, Brace, World, 1961.

Olsen, Donald. *The City as a Work of Art*. New Haven: Yale University Press, 1986.

Paris Guide par les Principaux Ecrivains et Artistes de la France. Lacroix et Verboeckhoven et Cie., editeurs. Paris: Librairie International, 1867.

Paris Guide. Introduction et Choix de Textes de Corinne Verdet. Paris: La Découverte, 1983.

Paris Nouveau Illustré. Journal périodique publié par *L'Illustration*, 1864–1872. Paris: Imprimerie de E. Martinez.

Paul-Levy, Françoise. *La Ville en Croix: De la Revolution de 1848 à la Renovation Haussmannienne*. Paris: Librairie des Méridiens, 1984.

Pevsner, Nikolaus. *An Outline of European Architecture*. England: Penguin Books, 1968.

Philippe, Jullian. *Le Style 2nd Empire*. Paris: Baschet, 1975.

Pinkney, David. *Napoleon III and the Re-building of Paris.* Princeton: Princeton University Press, 1958.

Reau, Louis. *L'Oeuvre du Baron Hauss-mann.* Paris: Presses Universitaires de France, 1954.

Reid, Donald. *Paris Sewers and Sewermen.* Cambridge, Mass.: Harvard University Press, 1991.

Rosenau, Helen. *Boullée and Visionary Architecture.* New York: Harmony Books, 1976.

Rouleau, Bernard. *Le Tracé des rues de Paris: Formation, Typologie, Fonc-tions.* Paris: Editions du Centre Na-tional de la Recherche Scientifique, 1983.

Saalman, H. *Haussmann: Paris Trans-formed.* New York: Braziller, 1971.

Sutcliffe, Anthony. *The Autumn of Central Paris.* London: E. Arnold, 1970.

Sutcliffe, Anthony, ed. *Metropolis.* Chicago: University of Chicago Press, 1984.

Suttel, René. *Catacombes et Carrières de Paris.* Paris: Editions SEHDACS, 1986.

Taxil, M. L. *Recueil des Actes Administra-tifs aux Servitudes Speciales d'Architec-ture,* publiée sous la direction de M. Bouvard. Paris, 1905.

de Thézy, Marie. *Paris, La Rue: Le Mobilier Urbain du 2nd Empire à Nos Jours.* Ex. cat. Bibliothèque Historique de la Ville de Paris. Paris, 1976.

Touttain, Pierre-André. *Haussmann: Artisan du Second Empire.* Paris: Librairie Grund, 1971.

Van Zanten, David. *Designing Paris.* Cam-bridge, Mass.: MIT Press, 1987.

Wisman, Heinz, ed. *Walter Benjamin et Paris, Colloque International, 25–29 Juin 1983.* Paris: Les Editions du Cerf, 1986.

French and Parisian Social History

Agulhon, Maurice. *1848 ou l'Apprentissage de la République 1848–1852.* Paris: Editions du Seuil, 1973.

Allen, Maurice. *La Vie Quotidienne Sous le Second Empire.* Paris: Hachette, 1948.

Ariès, Philippe. "Contribution à l'Etude du Culte des Morts à l'Epoque Conte-mporaine." *Essais sur l'Histoire de la Mort.* Paris: Seuil, 1975.

Ariès, Philippe. *The Hour of Our Death.* Trans. Helen Weaver. New York: Knopf, 1981.

Ariès, Philippe. *Western Attitudes Toward Death: From the Middle Ages to the Present*. Trans. Patricia M. Ranum. Baltimore: The Johns Hopkins Press, 1974.

Bon Marché. *Grands Magasins de Nouveautés au Bon Marché*. Catalogue c. 1874.

Bousquet, Charles. *La Garde Impériale au Camp de Châlons*. Paris: Imprimerie et Librairie Militaire de Blot, 1857.

Cameron, Rondo. *La France et la Développement Economique de l'Europe. 1800–1914*. Trans. Marianne Berthod. Paris: Editions du Seuil, 1971.

Chevalier, Louis. *Classes Laborieuses et Classes Dangereuses*. Paris: Hachette, 1984.

Chevalier, Louis. *La Formation de la Population Parisienne au 19ème Siècle*. Institut National d'Etudes Demographiques. Travaux et Documents Cahier 10. Paris: Presses Universitaires de France, 1950.

Clarétie, Jules. *Voyages d'un Parisien*. Paris: A. Faure, 1865.

Cobban, Alfred. *A History of Modern France*. 2 vols. Middlesex, England: Penguin, 1974.

Corbin, Alain. *Les Filles de Noce: Misère Sexuelle et Prostitution aux 19è et 20è Siècles*. Paris: Aubier Montaigne, 1978.

Corbin, Alain. *Le Miasme et la Jonquille*. Paris: Aubier, 1982.

Courtine, Robert. *La Vie Parisienne*. 3 vols. Paris: Librairie Académique Perrin, 1984.

Darnton, Robert. *The Literary Underground of the Old Regime*. Cambridge, Mass.: Harvard University Press, 1982.

Daumard, Adeline. *Les Bourgeois de Paris au XIXè Siècle*. Paris: Flammarion, 1970.

Dauzet, Pierre. *Le Siècle des Chemins de Fer en France 1821–1938*. Fontaney-aux-Roses: Imprimeries Bellenand, 1948.

DeFrance, M. Eugene. *Histoire de l'Eclairage des Rues de Paris*. Paris: Imprimerie Nationale, 1904.

Deleuze, Gilles, and Félix Guattari. *A Thousand Plateaus: Capitalism and Schizophrenia*. Trans. Brian Massumi. Minneapolis: University of Minnesota Press, 1987.

Derens, Jean, ed. *Métropolitain*. Ex. cat. Bibliothèque Historique de la Ville de Paris. Paris, 1988.

Le Diable à Paris. Texts by G. Sand, H. de Balzac, G. de Nerval, A. de Musset, T. Gautier, et al. Illustrated by Gavarni. 2 vols. Paris: J. Hetzel, 1845.

Du Camp, Maxime. *Paris: Ses Organes, Ses Fonctions et Sa Vie Dans La Seconde Moitié du XIXè Siècle,* 6 vols. Paris: Librairie Hachette, 1893.

Edwards, Stewart. *The Communards of Paris 1871*. Ithaca: Cornell University Press, 1973.

Farge, Arlette. *Vivre dans la Rue à Paris au XVIIIè Siècle*. Paris: Editions Gallimard/Julliard, 1979.

Favier, Jean et al. *Les Débuts du Chemin de Fer en France, 1831–1870*. Ex. cat. Musée de l'Histoire de France. Paris: Archives Nationales, 1977.

Fournel, Victor. *La Déportation des Morts*. Paris: Armand Le Chevalier, 1870.

Gastineau, Benjamin. *La Vie en Chemin de Fer*. Paris: E. Dentu, 1861.

Gautier, T., A. Dumas, A. Houssaye, A. de Musset, P. Enault, and L. Du Fayl. *Paris et les Parisiens au XIXè Siècle: Moeurs, Arts et Monuments*. Paris: Morizot, 1856.

Giedion, Siegfried. *Mechanization Takes Command*. New York: Norton Library, 1948.

Holtman, Robert B. *Napoleonic Propaganda*. New York: 1950.

Isay, Raymond. *Panorama des Expositions Universelles*. Paris: Gallimard, 1937.

Isser, Natalie. *The Second Empire and the Press*. The Hague: 1974.

Kellett, John R. *The Impact of Railways on Victorian Cities*. London: Routledge and Kegan Paul, 1969.

Laffont, Robert. *Panorama d'Histoire: Histoire de Paris et des Parisiens*. Paris: Editions Robert Laffont, 1958.

Lefevre, André. *Sous le Second Empire: Chemins de Fer et Politique*. Paris: SEDES, 1951.

Lefevre, Henri. *La Vie Quotidienne dans le Monde Moderne*. Paris: Gallimard, 1968.

Leri, Jean-Marc. *La Presse à Paris, 1851–1881*. Ex. cat. Bibliothèque Historique de la Ville de Paris. Paris, 1983.

Mareschal, Jules. *Les Chemins de Fer Considerés au Point de Vue Social et Civilisateur*. Paris: Librairie Hachette et Cie., 1854.

Merlin, Pierre. *Les Transports Parisiens*. Paris: Masson et Cie., 1967.

Miller, Michael B. *The Bon Marché: Bourgeois Culture and the Department Store 1869–1920*. Princeton: Princeton University Press, 1981.

Morin, Edgar. *L'Homme et la Mort*. Paris: Editions du Seuil, 1970.

Naud, M. Louis. *Histoire de la Télégraphie en France*. Paris: Bureaux du Courrier des Examens, 1890.

O'Brien, Patrick. *Railways and the Economic Development of Western Europe, 1830–1914*. New York: St. Martins Press, 1983.

Oster, Daniel, and Jean Goulemot. *La Vie Parisienne: Anthologie des Moeurs du XIXè Siècle*. Paris: Sand/Conti, 1989.

Parent-Duchâtelet, Alexandre. *La Prostitution à Paris Au XIXè Siècle*. Paris: Editions du Seuil, 1981.

Pinkney, David. *Decisive Years in France: 1840–1847*. Princeton: Princeton University Press, 1986.

Plessis, Alain. *De La Fête Impériale au Mur des Fédérés 1852–1871*. Paris: Editions du Seuil, 1979.

Poete, Marcel. *Une Vie de Cité: Paris de sa naissance à nos jours*. 3 vols. Paris: Auguste Picard, 1925.

Rancière, Jacques. *The Nights of Labor: The Worker's Dream in 19th Century France*. Trans. John Drury. Philadelphia: Temple University Press, 1989.

Rapport à La Société Positiviste Par la Commission Chargée d'Examiner la Nature et le Plan du Nouveau Gouvernement Révolutionnaire de la République Française. Paris: Librairie Scientifique-Industrielle de L. Mathias, 1848.

Richards, Jeffrey, and John MacKenzie. *The Railway Station: A Social History*. Oxford and New York: Oxford University Press, 1986.

Say, Leon. *La Ville de Paris et le Crédit Foncier*. Paris: Guillaumin et Cie./Dentu, 1868.

Schivelbusch, Wolfgang. *The Railway Journey*. Berkeley: University of California Press, 1986.

Sennett, Richard. *The Fall of Public Man: On the Social Psychology of Capitalism*. New York: Vintage Books, 1978.

Simmel, Georg. *The Sociology of Georg Simmel*. Trans. Kurt H. Wolff. London: Free Press of Glencoe, 1950.

Stilgoe, John R. *The Metropolitan Corridor*. New Haven and London: Yale University Press, 1983.

Sternberger, Dolf. *Panorama of the Nineteenth Century*. New York: Urizen Books, 1977.

Tester, Keith, ed. *The Flâneur*. London: Routledge, 1994.

Texier, Edmond. *Tableau de Paris*. Paris: Paulin et le Chevalier, 1852.

Thompson J. M. *Louis Napoleon and the Second Empire*. New York: Columbia University Press, 1983.

Vigarello, Georges. *Le Propre et le Sale: l'Hygiène du Corps depuis le Moyen Age*. Paris: Editions du Seuil, 1985.

Vincenot, Henri. *La Vie Quotidienne dans les Chemins de Fer au XIXè Siècle*. Paris: Hachette, 1975.

Wexler, Peter. *La Formation du Vocabulaire des Chemins de Fer en France, 1778–1842*. Geneve: Librairie E. Droz, 1955.

Williams, Roger L. *Gaslight and Shadow: The World of Napoleon 3, 1851– 1870.* New York: Macmillan, 1957.

Williams, Rosalind. *Dream Worlds: Mass Consumption in Late 19th Century France.* Berkeley: University of California Press, 1982.

d'Ydewalle, Charles. *Au Bon Marché: de la Boutique au Grand Magasin.* Paris: Librairie Plon, 1965.

Selected Works on Art, Literature, and Cultural History

There is no way to list all of the works that allow a scholar to "perceive" a cultural era. Much of my knowledge of this period comes directly from its primary cultural sources: from the novels of Balzac, Hugo, Flaubert, and Zola, from the poetry and criticism of Baudelaire and Gautier; from the paintings of Manet, Degas, Monet, Courbet, and their colleagues, for example. The works listed here, therefore, are those that add to the continuing dialogue about these creative sources—which frame and reframe our vision of art, life, and their uneasy relationship in France during the Second Empire.

Adams, Robert Martin. *NIL: Episodes in the Literary Conquest of Void during the 19th century.* New York: Oxford University Press, 1966.

Auerbach, Erich. *Mimesis.* Trans. Willard R. Trask. Princeton: Princeton University Press, 1953.

Aumont, Jacques. *L'oeil Interminable: Cinéma et Peinture.* Paris: Librairie Séguier, 1989.

de Balzac, Honoré. *Les Parisiens Comme Ils Sont, 1830–1846.* Genève: La Palatine, 1947.

Bann, Stephen. *The Clothing of Clio: A Study of the Representation of History in 19th Century Britain and France.* Cambridge: Cambridge University Press, 1984.

Bapst, Germain. *Essai sur l'Histoire des Panoramas et des Dioramas.* Paris: Imprimerie Nationale/Librairie G. Masson, 1891.

Baudelaire, Charles. *Art in Paris 1845– 1862.* Trans. and ed. Jonathan Mayne. Ithaca, N.Y.: Cornell/Phaidon Books, Cornell University Press, 1981.

Baudelaire, Charles. *The Painter of Modern Life and Other Essays*. Trans. and ed. Jonathan Mayne. New York: Phaidon, 1970.

Benjamin, Walter. *Charles Baudelaire: A Lyric Poet in the Era of High Capitalism*. London: Verso Editions, 1976.

Berman, Marshall. *All That Is Solid Melts into Air*. New York: Simon and Schuster, 1982.

Bersani, Leo. *Baudelaire and Freud*. Berkeley: University of California Press, Quantum Books, 1977.

Boime, Albert. *The Academy and French Painting in the 19th Century*. New Haven: Yale University Press, 1986.

Clark, T. J. *The Absolute Bourgeois: Artists and Politics in France 1848–1851*. Princeton: Princeton University Press, 1982.

Clark, T. J. *The Image of the People: Gustave Courbet and the 1848 Revolution*. Princeton: Princeton University Press, 1982.

Clark, T. J. *The Painting of Modern Life*. New York: Knopf, 1984.

Comment, Bernard. *Le XIXè Siècle des Panoramas*. Paris: Adam Biro, 1983.

Coven, Jeffrey. *Baudelaire's Voyages*. Ex. cat. Heckscher Museum. New York: Bulfinch, 1993.

Crow, Thomas E. *Painters and Public Life in 18th century Paris*. New Haven: Yale University Press, 1985.

Delacroix, E. *The Journal of Eugène Delacroix*. Trans. Walter Pach. New York: Viking, 1972.

Fruiteman, E. J., and Paul A. Zoetmulder. *The Panoramas Phenomena. Mesdag Panoramas, 1881–1981*. Ex. cat. The Hague, 1981.

de Goncourt, Edmond and Jules. *The Goncourt Journals 1851–1870*. New York: Doubleday, 1937.

Hamilton, George Heard. *Manet and His Critics*. New York: Norton Library, 1969.

Herbert, Robert. *Impressionism*. New Haven: Yale University Press, 1989.

Hyde, Ralph. *Panoramania*. London: Barbican Art Gallery, 1988.

Holt, Elizabeth Gilmore. *The Triumph of Art for the Public*. New York: Anchor Books, 1979.

Kern, Stephen. *The Culture of Time and Space, 1880–1918*. Cambridge, Mass.: Harvard University Press, 1983.

Klingender, F. D. *Art and the Industrial Revolution*. New York: Schocken, 1970.

Kraucauer, S. *Jacques Offenbach: ou le Secret du Second Empire*. Paris: Editions Bernard Grasset, 1937.

Marx, Leo. *The Machine in the Garden.* New York: Oxford University Press, 1964.

Littré, Emile. *Auguste Comte et la Philosophie Positive.* Paris: Librairie de la Hachette et Cie., 1863.

Mainardi, Patricia. *Art and Politics of the Second Empire.* New Haven: Yale University Press, 1987.

Marrinan, Michael. *Painting Politics for Louis-Philippe: Art and Ideology in Orléanist France.* New Haven: Yale University Press, 1988.

Max, Stefan. *Les Metamorphoses de la Grande Ville dans les Rougon-Macquart.* Paris: Librairie A. G. Nizet, 1966.

Mead, George. *Movements of Thought in the 19th Century.* Chicago: University of Chicago Press, 1967.

Minkowski, M. "Le Problème du Temps Vécu." *Recherches Philosophiques* 5. Paris: Librairie Bovin et Cie. (1935–6): 65–99.

de Nerval, Gerard. *Paris et Alentours.* Paris: Encre, 1980.

Nochlin, Linda, ed. *Impressionism and Post-Impressionism, 1874–1904.* New York: Prentice Hall, 1966.

Nochlin, Linda. *The Politics of Vision: Essays on Nineteenth Century Art and Society.* New York: Harper and Row, 1989.

Nochlin, Linda. *Realism.* Baltimore: Penguin Books, 1971.

Nodier, M. Charles et al. *Paris Historique: Promenade dans les Rues de Paris.* Tomes 1 et 2. Paris: F. G. Lourault, 1838.

Novak, Barbara. *Nature and Culture.* New York: Oxford University Press, 1980.

Novotny, Fritz. *Painting and Sculpture in Europe, 1780–1880.* Baltimore: Pelican History of Art, 1971.

Pichois, Claude, et Jean-Paul Avice. *Baudelaire/Paris.* Ex. cat. Bibliothèque Historique de la Ville de Paris. Paris: Editions Paris-Musées, 1993.

Rollet, Patrice. "Passage des Panoramas." In *Paris Vu Par Le Cinéma d'Avant-Garde.* Ex. cat. Centre Pompidou. Paris, 1985.

Rosenblum, Robert, and H. W. Janson. *19th Century Art.* New York: Abrams, 1984.

Rosenblum, Robert. *Transformations in Late 18th Century Art.* Princeton: Princeton University Press, 1969.

Sartre, Jean-Paul. *Baudelaire.* New York: New Directions, 1950.

Second Empire: Art in France Under Napoleon III. Ex. cat. Philadelphia Museum of Art. Philadelphia, 1978.

*Sehsucht: Das Panorama Als Massenunter-
haltung des 19. Jahrhunderts.* Ex. cat.
Kunst and Austellungeshalle der
Bundesrepublik Deutschland. Bonn,
1993.

Shattuck, Roger. *Proust's Binoculars.*
Princeton: Princeton University Press,
1983.

Sheon, Aaron. "French Art and Science in
the Mid 19th Century: Some Points
of Contact." *Art Quarterly* (Winter
1971): 434–455.

Sheon, Aaron, "Parisian Social Statistics:
Gavarni, *Le Diable à Paris,* and Early
Realism." *Art Journal* 44, no. 2, 139–
148.

Siegel, Jerrold. *Bohemian Paris.* New York:
Viking, 1986.

Silvestre, Israel. *Vues de Paris.* Paris: Berger-
Levrault, 1977.

Straus, Erwin. "Le Mouvement Vécu." In
Recherches Philosophiques, no. 5.
Paris: Librairie Boivin et Cie. (1935–
6): 112–138.

Straus, Erwin. *The Primary World of the
Senses.* New York: MacMillan, 1966.

Trans-Cinéma-Express. *Une Rétrospective
des Films sur le Train.* Ex. cat. Le Centre Culturel de la Communauté Française de Belgique à Paris. Paris: 1981.

Tucker, Paul Hayes. *Monet at Argenteuil.*
New Haven: Yale University Press,
1982.

Varnedoe, K. *Gustave Caillebotte.* New
Haven: Yale University Press, 1984.

Varnedoe, K. "The Artifice of Candor: Impressionism and Photography Recon-
sidered." *Art in America* (Jan. 1980):
66–78.

Varnedoe, K. "The Ideology of Time." *Art
in America* (Summer 1980): 96–110.

Vogt, A. M. *Art of the Nineteenth Century.*
Trans. A. F. Bance. New York: Universe Books, 1973.

Wechsler, Judith. *A Human Comedy: Physi-
ognomy and Caricature in 19th Century Paris.* Chicago: University of
Chicago Press, 1982.

Index

Illustrations are in italics.

Balloons, hot air, 12, 18, 28, 127, 141, 147, 174, 178, 216. *See also* Aerial photography;
     Nadar
     "Le Géant," 172, *173.*
Balzac, Honoré de, 8, 9, 12, 32, 63, 70, 71, 75, 76, 82
     Les Petits Bourgeois, 12
     Splendeurs et Misères des Courtisane, 75
Barker, Robert, 127, 185
Barrière Blanche, 24; *25*
Barthes, Roland, 8, 10, 13, 17, 19, 145, 180
Bastille, 106
Baudelaire, Charles Pierre, 7, 8, 16, 41, 45, 53, 54, 67, 69, 74, 141, 147, 148, 158, 207, 214,
     224, 225; *149*
     "In Passing," 113–117
     "The Eyes of the Poor," 32–37, 57, 71, 82
     "The Painter of Modern Life," 151, 208
     "The Swan," 24–27, 179, 183
     "Travelers," 190–192, 193
Baudry. *See* Gide and Baudry
Bayard, Hippolyte, 6, 52, 88, 130; *77, 90, 128, 129*
Belgrand, Eugène, 44, 166
Benjamin, Walter, 8, 10, 16, 37, 38, 50, 51, 69, 74, 144, 148, 152, 184, 225
Bergson, Henri, 6
Bernhardt, Sarah, 148; *150*
Bertsch, Auguste, 24; *25*
La Bête Humaine, 109–110. *See also* Zola, E.
Bibliothèque Historique de la Ville de Paris, 12
Bisson Brothers, Louis-Auguste and Auguste-Rosalie, 130; *39, 131, 187*
Blanc, Charles, 48, 50
Blanc, Louis, 144, 151, 178
Blanquart-Evrard, Louis-Désiré, 46–47, 488, 52, 53, 88; *49, 132, 185*
La Bohème, 8
Bois de Boulogne, 101
Au Bonheur des Dames, 191. *See also* Zola, E.
Bon Marché, 38. *See also* Department stores
Bordeaux, 214; *213*
Boullée, Etienne-Louis, 174